God bless you, R~

LORD SRI KRISHNA'S COMMANDMENTS

Timeless secrets extracted from priceless scriptures

For Success, Happiness, Peace, Prosperity and Liberation

Raghuvamshi

Authentic, Spiritual and Scientific. Nothing religious about it.

Vinayak Raghuvamshi

(KRSNADAASA)

Lord Sri Krishna's Commandments

tellwell

Tellwell Talent
www.tellwell.ca

ISBN
978-1-77370-434-0 (Hardcover)
978-1-77370-433-3 (Paperback)
978-1-77370-435-7 (eBook)

Table of Contents

Introduction, Preface, And Context

This is a book by a common person for the common population in pursuit of eternal joy and liberation. The content of this book is primarily derived from the timeless wisdom contained in the 'Bhagavad Gita'[1].

I am an independent author, not affiliated with any religious or political organization. I have focused only on extracting the actionable items or 'commandments' from this scripture. I have not made any attempts to re-interpret or provide my own version of the meaning of the verses contained in this scripture. Many great scholars like Swami Ranganathananda, Bhakti Vedanta Swami Prabhupada, Swami Vivekananda, Bal Gangadhar Tilak, Swami Sankaracharya, Georg Feuerstein etc. have all provided excellent interpretations. These are the works that I have drawn inspiration from.

So, why did I come out with this book?

Although there is an ocean of wisdom in the Bhagavad Gita, it takes a lot of time, efforts, peace of mind and guidance to go through

1 The Bhagavad Gita is also just called 'Gita'. More details here: https://en.wikipedia.org/wiki/Bhagavad_Gita

and comprehend. Many of us live hectic and stressful lives. We need some tips and guidelines for breaking away from this hectic routine, achieve financial stability and attain some peace of mind. We then can spend all our time and energy on diving deep into such scriptures and progressing on the path to spiritual success leading to liberation.

What we need first is a set of guidelines or 'commandments' which would help us succeed in this material life while progressing gradually in the spiritual plane to reach the point wherein we start having a direct connection with God.

Take the example of a child. When she is trying to touch the fire, you must give her a commandment that says 'never touch fire'. The child may want to understand 'why' but the top priority here is that she stays safe. It is absolutely important that the child gets such meaningful commandments that she can follow, in order to stay safe and grow up to be a healthy human being. Once she grows up, she can then spend all the time she wants on studying and getting an in-depth understanding of all the aspects of fire and other elements in nature. What is very important is that we all have a set of strong guidelines or commandments that will guide us towards a successful life.

This is my humble attempt to extract the commandments from the Gita. I have gone through multiple scholarly works as quoted above to pick the best explanation of the shlokas [2]/ verses in the context of the commandment that follows. I have used only those shlokas that provide a context for the commandments and I encourage the reader to look up the shloka from any version of Gita that he/she prefers to get a deeper understanding of the same.

The Sanskrit shlokas are provided only for context and authenticity. You do not need to be able to read them although the English literals are also provided under each shloka for reference.

---

2 Shloka is a Sanskrit word for 'verse' or 'hymn'

There are many Sanskrit words that have been interpreted a bit differently by each scholar. For example, let's take the simple word 'snigdha' from the verse 17.8. This has been translated as "rich-in-oil" by Georg Feuerstein, "soft" by Dr. Radhakrishnan, "fatty" by Bhakti Vedanta Swami Pabhupada. Another example is with a more serious word "dharma" as it appears in verse 3.35, which is interpreted by Sri Prabhupada as "duties", Georg Feuerstein as "life-laws", Swami Ranganathananda as "way of life" etc.

For each verse, I have picked the most relevant interpretation based on the context and best fitment for the commandment / actionable items that we are extracting from the verse. Nowhere have I tried to introduce my own interpretation of any shloka or verse.

This ensures the authenticity of the text. I have only added additional context, explanations, examples and actionable commandments wherever applicable.

I would like to quote Sir Isaac Newton who famously said: **"If I have seen further it is by standing on ye shoulders of giants**".

I share the same feeling and I would like to specifically call out these scholarly giants below.

Here are the four major scholars whose works have inspired me and guided me:

1. **Swami Ranganathananda**: He provides very deep analysis and a lot of context for each verse. He is a Vedanta scholar and a proponent of Advaita[3] (non-duality) philosophy. He is a master storyteller and provides references from such varied sources which is truly commendable.
2. **Swami Bhakti Vedanta Prabhupada**: Needless to say, he is the most popular scholar when it comes to the Bhagavad

3 Advaita means non-dualistic and is a philosophy that says the same God is everywhere including inside you. You can read more about this here: https://en.wikipedia.org/wiki/Advaita_Vedanta

Gita and his version of Gita 'As It Is[4]' is the most widely read version on the planet. He single-handedly spread awareness about Lord Krishna's teachings in modern times and thanks to him, millions have got easy access to the wisdom contained in this timeless manuscript. His works emphasize a lot on bhakti yoga (yoga of devotion).

3. **Swami Vivekananda**: His lectures on the Gita are intellectually most stimulating and provide the most logical explanations. The complete works of Vivekananda [5]is a masterpiece on spirituality that every intellectual seeker should study.
4. **Georg Feuerstein**: This German scholar provides the most 'accurate' letter by letter interpretation of the verses. His works have helped me resolve ambiguity whenever I was faced with very different if not conflicting interpretations of the same word by multiple scholars.

I do want to clarify that although I have used the interpretations from these texts, I have not 'copy-pasted' or blindly reproduced any of their works at any place.

I am confident that these commandments will help you achieve success, peace, prosperity, and liberation. **The descriptions and commandments in this book are totally spiritual and scientific.** There is nothing religious about this book so I hope everyone can read it with an open mind and benefit from it.

Lord Krishna has reiterated many times that He and God are the same. So, wherever He uses the term 'I' or 'Me', we can replace it with 'God' and it should not make any difference to the meaning of the verse.

If you believe that Lord Krishna is God, then this should be perfectly fine as we are using the term 'God' and it implies Krishna only.

---

4 https://www.asitis.com/

5 http://www.ramakrishnavivekananda.info/vivekananda/complete_works.htm

If you don't believe that Lord Krishna is God, then using the term 'God' should be fine too, because then we are stressing on the spirit of what Lord Krishna is saying and focusing on the ultimate 'God'.

In my humble opinion, the world would be a much more peaceful place if everybody focused on the spirit of God rather than the name and form of God.

I would like to mention here that I received divine inspiration to write this book and I wholeheartedly believe that I am just an instrument while it is the divine forces who actually helped bring out the commandments through me. Forever indebted to all the divine entities who are always guiding me on my own path to liberation and union with the dear Supreme Lord.

God bless!

CHAPTER 1
The Saboteur Within

Each one of us has a good voice and a bad voice within us. We have all experienced multiple instances where one voice tells us to do the right thing while there is another voice that keeps tempting us to do mischievous or negative things.

Along with the bad voice, each one of us also has a saboteur within us. This is the entity that often prevents us from succeeding or being happy or peaceful in life.

Saboteur basically means 'one who causes sabotage'. In this case, we are talking about that entity within us that is hell-bent on sabotaging our own selves and constantly pushing us towards the path to failure and downfall.

Each of us must have faced the 'exam fever' many times in our lives. The good voice within us keeps saying 'you should stop wasting time and study'. While the saboteur keeps teasing us 'hey there is still a lot of time for the exam, let's play for some time or sleep for some time'. Sounds familiar? On a more serious note, there are countless criminals who break down at the time of their trials, saying 'I don't know what came over me. I was not myself. I can't believe I did that'. Well, they are speaking the truth and only describing the painful reality of having been victimized by their own inner saboteur.

Arjuna's[6] state of mind during the first few hours on the battlefield of Kurukshetra [7]is a perfect example of this saboteur in action.

One important thing to keep in mind is that, whenever you face the urge from negative feelings and emotions, you should make sure that they do not land up controlling your actions.

The mystic and saint Kabir [8]explains this beautifully in two lines:

मन गया तो जाने दे, मत जाने दे शरीर।

बिन चिल्ले चढ़ी कमान, किस बिध लागे तीर?

Man gaya tho jaane de, math jaane de shareer.

Bin chille chadi kamaan, kis bidh lage teer?

Which means: If your mind wanders, let it. But do not let your body follow your mind (do not act on what the wandering mind is thinking about). It is like a bow which is stretched to its full limit, but without an arrow (body) it can do no harm.

In the context of the setting for Bhagavad Gita, Arjuna's mind is playing the reverse trick and forcing him into total inaction. Either way, be it action or inaction, we should not let the wandering mind dictate the terms.

Arjuna advertises this state of his mind as described at the end of the first chapter of Bhagavad Gita.

There are two central themes of the first chapter in the Bhagavad Gita.

---

6 Arjuna was the most celebrated warrior and archer of his times. He was dear to the Lord and the entire Bhagavad Gita was recited to him directly by Lord Krishna on the battlefield of Kurukshetra

7 Kurukshetra was the battlefield where the epic battle of Mahabharata took place between the virtuous Pandavas and evil Kauravas.

8 Kabir was a 15th century spiritual master and saint as well as renowned poet, very popular for his two line poems called 'dohas'.

1. Deal with the saboteur within and fight the weakness of mind
2. Realize that the body is temporary while the soul is eternal. Do not grieve for the body.

यदि मामप्रतीकारमशस्त्रं शस्त्रपाणयः ।
धार्तराष्ट्रा रणे हन्युस्तन्मे क्षेमतरं भवेत् ॥ १-४६ ॥

yadi mām apratīkāram aśastraṃ śastrapāṇayaḥ ।
dhārtarāṣṭrā raṇe hanyus tan me kṣemataraṃ bhavet ॥1-46॥

It would be better for me even if the sons of Dhritarashtra[9], *weapons in hand, kill me on the battlefield while I am unarmed and unresisting.*

Such words coming from the most feared warrior of his times is a classic example of the saboteur within him fully in action. Lord Sri Krishna addresses this saboteur within Arjuna directly in the next chapter.

9 *Dhritarashtra* was the blind king and father of the evil Kauravas

CHAPTER 2
Managing Our Negative Mind

कुतस्त्वा कश्मलमिदं विषमे समुपस्थितम् ।
अनार्यजुष्टमस्वर्ग्यमकीर्तिकरमर्जुन ॥२-२॥

kutas tvā kaśmalam idaṃ viṣame samupasthitam ।
anāryajuṣṭam asvargyam akīrtikaram arjuna ॥2-2॥

Arjuna! from where have these impurities (dirtiness) come unto you at this crucial time (hour of crisis)? They are not befitting a person who knows the value of life. Such Behavior does not lead to higher planets. They only lead to loss of keerthi[10] *and cause infamy.*

One of the major problems with this saboteur within us is that it often comes across as being your friend and will make very intelligent and logical arguments that sound convincing and even virtuous at times. And it will do this at the most crucial time when it is most destructive to you.

Unless we have a pure heart and the grace of the Lord it is extremely difficult to even realize that it is your inner saboteur that is causing you failure and pain most of the times.

10 Keerthi here means fame or glory

It becomes extremely difficult to distinguish your saboteur from your good voice and well-wisher. Even a wise, pious, ethical, strong and fierce warrior like Arjuna can become a victim of this cunning saboteur.

Krishna then reprimands this saboteur within Arjuna and commands him thus:

क्लैब्यं मा स्म गमः पार्थ नैतत्त्वय्युपपद्यते ।
क्षुद्रं हृदयदौर्बल्यं त्यक्त्वोत्तिष्ठ परंतप ॥२-३॥

klaibyaṃ mā sma gamaḥ pārtha naitat tvayy upapadyate ।
kṣudraṃ hṛdayadaurbalyaṃ tyaktvottiṣṭha paraṃtapa ॥2-3॥

Do not yield to this impotence, O Partha[11]*! Such behavior is not befitting of you. Give up such petty weakness of heart and arise! O chastiser of the enemy!*

Based on the discussions till here, we can extract the first commandment of Lord Sri Krishna.

Commandment 1:

Recognize the saboteur within you. Don't give into it. Confront it and vanquish it.

The best way to accomplish this is by paying attention to your thoughts. The moment you catch yourself trying to do or say negative or harmful things, realize that it is your inner saboteur in action. The very act of being caught in action is enough to make your saboteur go back into hiding. Every criminal is afraid of being caught. It is the same with your inner saboteur. Keep catching it in action and it will eventually become inactive and dormant.

---

11 Partha is Arjuna, the son of Pritha which is another name for his mother Kunti.

मात्रास्पर्शास्तु कौन्तेय शीतोष्णसुखदुःखदाः ।
आगमापायिनोऽनित्यास्तांस्तितिक्षस्व भारत ॥२-१४॥

mātrāsparśās tu kaunteya śītoṣṇasukhaduḥkhadāḥ I
āgamāpāyino 'nityās tāṃs titikṣasva bhārata II2-14II

Dualities like happiness & sadness, summer & winter, etc. are a result of sensory perceptions and are very temporary. You should learn to tolerate them, O descendant of Bharatha[12]!

यं हि न व्यथयन्त्येते पुरुषं पुरुषर्षभ ।
समदुःखसुखं धीरं सोऽमृतत्वाय कल्पते ॥२-१५॥

yaṃ hi na vyathayanty ete puruṣaṃ puruṣarṣabha I
samaduḥkhasukhaṃ dhīraṃ so 'mṛtatvāya kalpate II2-15II

O best among men, he who is not disturbed by happiness & distress and is steady in both is certainly eligible for liberation.

Commandment 2:

A calm mind is essential for achieving liberation. Learn to handle both pain and pleasure calmly.

This does not mean that you become totally emotionless. It is OK to feel happy or sad. You should just not get too excited in good times or too agitated during bad times. The easiest way to achieve this is to always tell yourself that "even this will pass". This applies to both good as well as bad times and will help you stay grounded and calm under all situations.

When you are feeling very emotional, regardless of whether it is positive or negative emotions, do not say or do anything impulsively.

12 Bharatha was a great emperor and founder of Bharath (modern day India). He is the ancestor of both, Pandavas as well as Kauravas.

Because whatever you do or say will not be appropriate or in your best interests.

Here is a wonderful example from the Ramayana[13]. Lord Rama's father, the great king Dasharatha was once rescued from the battlefield by his wife Kaikeyi. It was quite natural for him to feel grateful and thankful. However, brimming with extreme emotion, he promises Kaikeyi that he will grant her 'any two wishes'. This promise is what lands up causing him to lose his sons Rama and Lakshmana along with his daughter-in-law Sita. It was his emotion that made the promise, not his intellect. This one mistake committed in a state of extreme emotion laid the foundation of an entire epic called Ramayana.

This was an example where someone acted unwisely in a state of extreme positive emotion. Likewise, here is an example where someone committed a blunder in a state of negative emotion (anger, rage).

King Parikshit, the son of Abhimanyu, inherited the kingdom of the Kurus after the Pandavas. True to his lineage, he was a valorous warrior, just monarch and adored by his subjects. He was very fond of hunting for sport.

One day, while hunting in the forest, he was separated from his followers and got lost. He wandered around, in search of water to quench his thirst, but did not find any. In this emaciated state, deep in the woods, he came across a humble hermitage. A high-souled rishi[14] was sitting in a posture of meditation below a nearby tree. He went near the rishi and humbly requested him for food and water.

The rishi was observing an oath of silence, which prevented him from even trying to communicate with the king. He remained

---

13 The Ramayana is one of the largest ancient epics in world literature. It is a story about the triumph of good over evil.

14 rishi is another term for a sage

deep in meditation. The king was extremely angry. He saw that a dead snake was lying in the grass nearby. He garlanded the rishi with this unclean object. After offering this insult, he went his way. Throughout this, the rishi remained silent, continuing his meditation.

When the rishi's son Sringin found out about this, he was extremely angry and cursed the king, saying, "Since out of the arrogance of his power, Parikshit has garlanded my father with a dead snake, may he die before the seventh day from today, bitten by a snake. The impious king shall be sent to the abode of death by the king of the serpents. Thus shall the king meet with an untimely death!"

When the rishi heard about this, he was sad and shocked. He called his son to his abode, and said, "Son, When I myself have forgiven king Parikshit for the insult offered, why did you curse him? Do you not know that he is a just and illustrious king? He was tired and hungry that day and committed this venial offense in a fit of rage. Except for this one instance, he has been an exemplary ruler. Thanks to his just rule, the rishis can continue their penances without fear of interruption. **It behooves a learned person to keep his anger and passion under strict control**. It is evident that you are yet to reach the mental maturity required to become an ascetic. Your education is, therefore, incomplete. Go to the forest and learn to control your anger by indulging in constant penance!".

If someone hurts you and you are feeling anger or resentment, do not say something harsh because you cannot take back your words or actions and you can only repent later on. As you can see, even one promise made in excitement or one blunder committed in anger can cost you dearly in life.

This is what this commandment is about. Stay calm in the face of both kinds of emotions and always use your intellect to make right choices.

कर्मण्येवाधिकारस्ते मा फलेषु कदा चन ।
मा कर्मफलहेतुर्भूर्मा ते सङ्गो ऽस्त्वकर्मणि ॥२-४७॥

karmaṇy evādhikāras te mā phaleṣu kadā cana |
mā karmaphalahetur bhūr mā te saṅgo 'stv akarmaṇi ||2-47||

You are entitled to (or have a right to) perform rightful actions. But you are never entitled to the fruits of your action. Never be motivated by the fruits of actions nor be attached to inaction.

This is one of the most iconic verses of the Bhagavad Gita and has been quoted countless times by many seers, sages, and scholars since time immemorial.

This is also the central idea behind most other teachings in the Gita. We are instructed by the Lord to always focus on our duties and rightful actions. All sorts of anxiety and stress occur only when we fret about the results of our actions. We all have that one friend or relative who is always depressed, feeling 'I did so much for everybody or I have given so much, but what have I received in return?'. The happiest people are those who never seek or worry about credit for their actions. They just do what they think is right and then move on.

Detachment from results is the way to a happy and painless life.

Commandment 3:

Always choose rightful action over inaction. Never be attached to the results of your work.

If you reflect on your own life you will realize that most of your painful memories are based on either something unexpected happening or something expected not happening. 'Expectation' is always the cause. Many western and eastern philosophers have established this fact over and over again.

Even in Buddha's teachings, one of the Four Noble Truths[15] is that "**the cause of all sufferings is attachment**".

If you look at nature, you see such detached actions everywhere. The honeybees gather honey but have you ever come across a honeybee which was looking depressed because someone else was enjoying the honey that it gathered? Have you ever come across a hummingbird which stopped singing because nobody was listening?

It becomes easier to practice commandment 3 when you have gained some mastery over the first two commandments. Your good self (higher self) always wants to do good deeds. However, your saboteur within will either prevent you from doing them or it will make you feel bad about doing good deeds by making you focus on the results of your actions.

ध्यायतो विषयान्पुंसः सङ्गस्तेषूपजायते ।
सङ्गात्संजायते कामः कामात्क्रोधो ऽभिजायते ॥२-६२॥

dhyāyato viṣayān puṃsaḥ saṅgas teṣūpajāyate I
saṅgāt saṃjāyate kāmaḥ kāmāt krodho 'bhijāyate II2-62II

While contemplating upon objects of the senses, a person develops attachment for them and from attachment lust develops and from lust, anger arises.

15 https://en.wikipedia.org/wiki/Four_Noble_Truths

Lord Krishna demonstrates his 'Cosmic scientist' side in this and the next phrases. In these, he lays down the perils to avoid and the perilous outcomes in a very objective, cause-effect manner.

A key point to be noted is that lust is not just about sexual attraction. Any sensory attachment, when it becomes so strong that you feel you cannot live without it, is termed as lust. Unfulfilled lust always leads to anger. And you can never fulfill lust because, by definition, lust is insatiable.

Trying to satisfy your lust by fulfilling it is like trying to satisfy or quell a fire by pouring more oil into it. So, invariably, lust leads to disappointment and anger.

Lord Krishna's Formula 1:

Thinking about sensory objects → Leads to attachment.
Attachment → Leads to lust.
Lust → Leads to anger.

क्रोधाद्भवति संमोहः संमोहात्स्मृतिविभ्रमः ।
स्मृतिभ्रंशाद्बुद्धिनाशो बुद्धिनाशात्प्रणश्यति ॥२-६३॥

krodhād bhavati saṃmohaḥ saṃmohāt smṛtivibhramaḥ ।
smṛtibhraṃśād buddhināśo buddhināśāt praṇaśyati ॥2-63॥

From anger, delusion arises which in turn leads to damage of memory. A damaged memory impacts intelligence. When intelligence is lost, it causes one to fall down (to lower planes).

Lord Krishna's Formula 2:

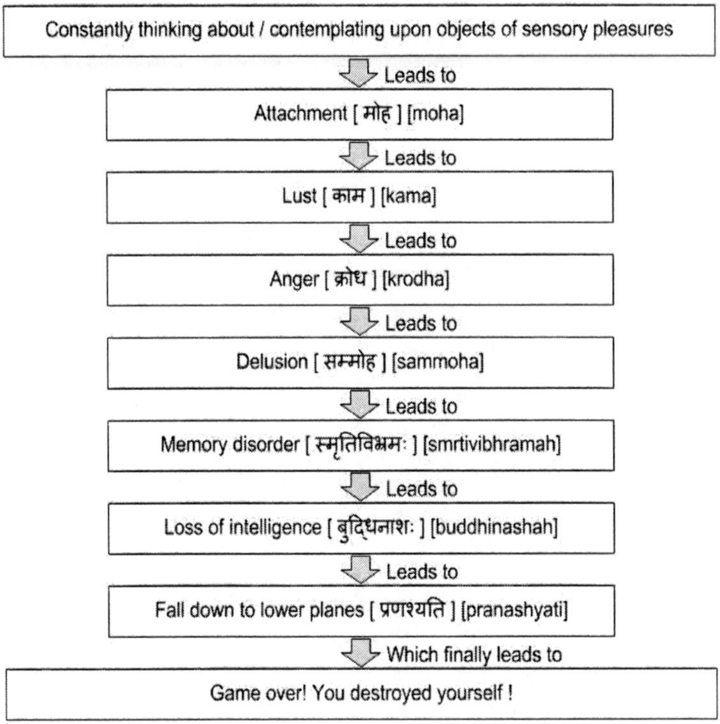

Commandment 4:

Let thoughts of God & service to God replace your thoughts of sensory pleasures.

In my humble opinion, it is very difficult to escape once you're caught in the vicious cycles of cause and effect. So it is best to take measures to avoid the root cause of your problem which is contemplating upon objects of sensory pleasures. And the easiest way to achieve this is by replacing such thoughts with the thoughts of God and how you can serve Him.

There are so many movies and novels about tragic stories that all begin with a man merely glancing upon a woman (or vice versa). Then soon he starts thinking about that woman all the time. And then he starts feeling like he just cannot live without that woman (although he has lived all these years without her). Then starts all the trouble. He tries hard to get that woman. When he is unable to get her, he gets angry and depressed and from that point on, there is only sadness and destruction.

There is a very interesting and insightful story that is often taught by Zen masters. It goes like this:

A senior monk and a junior monk were traveling together. At one point, they came to a river with a strong current. As the monks were preparing to cross the river, they saw a very young and beautiful woman also attempting to cross. The young woman asked if they could help her cross to the other side.

The two monks glanced at one another because they had taken vows not to touch a woman.

Then, without a word, the older monk picked up the woman, carried her across the river, placed her gently on the other side, and carried on with his journey.

The younger monk couldn't believe what had just happened. After rejoining his companion, he was speechless, and an hour passed without a word between them.

Two more hours passed, then three, finally the younger monk could not contain himself any longer, and confronted the older monk "As monks, we are not permitted to touch a woman, how could you then carry that woman on your shoulders?"

The older monk looked at him and replied, "Brother, I set her down on the other side of the river many hours ago, why are you still carrying her?"

Such a beautiful lesson. The problem is not with the sensory objects themselves. The problem is when we start contemplating upon or thinking upon those sensory objects.

Once our attention is caught by some such sensory objects (people or things), it is futile to try and fight those thoughts. Because doesn't matter whether you say 'I want' or 'I don't want', either way, you land up focusing on the object that you want or don't want. So, trying to fight those thoughts only makes those thoughts stronger.

Instead, the trick that Lord Krishna explains is to 'replace' those thoughts with the thoughts of God and service to God. Every time a name comes to your mind, replace it with the name of God, every time a face comes to your mind, replace it with the face of the Lord. That is the best and only way to escape from the clutches of all self-destructive thoughts.

नास्ति बुद्धिरयुक्तस्य न चायुक्तस्य भावना ।
न चाभावयतः शान्तिरशान्तस्य कुतः सुखम् ॥२-६६॥

nāsti buddhir ayuktasya na cāyuktasya bhāvanā I
na cābhāvayataḥ śāntir aśāntasya kutaḥ sukham II2-66II

There is no wisdom faculty for the unyoked[16]*. And for the unyoked, there is also no becoming-whole which implies a lack of peace, and happiness can't come to someone who is not peaceful.*

Humans domesticate animals by tying them to a tree or a pole to prevent them from running wild. Lord Krishna says that our senses also need to be domesticated similarly, to make sure that they don't run wild.

The best way to domesticate our senses is by tying them to God consciousness. In the spiritual sense, the yoke or the controlling force would be our connection with the Supreme and our connection with our higher, inner self.

Once we establish this connection, the senses can be domesticated. This is the only effective and sustainable way to control our senses which is crucial for achieving liberation.

Focus your thoughts on the Lord and tie your senses to the yoke of God consciousness. This is the key to liberation.

---

16 Yoking is the act of tying an animal to a pole or tree

CHAPTER 3

Karma Yoga, The Yoga Of Action

न कर्मणामनारम्भान्नैष्कर्म्यं पुरुषो ऽश्नुते ।
न च संन्यसनादेव सिद्धिं समधिगच्छति ॥ ३-४ ॥

na karmaṇām anārambhān naiṣkarmyaṃ puruṣo 'śnute I
na ca saṃnyasanād eva siddhiṃ samadhigacchati II3-4II

You cannot achieve freedom from the law of action and reaction merely by abstaining from work, nor can you attain perfection just by renunciation.

Here Sri Krishna clearly says that we cannot escape from the cycle of cause and effect by merely choosing to not act at all. Thus it is very important for us to understand the law of karma and seek the Lord's grace in helping us get liberation from this material world and its karmic cycles.

तस्मादसक्तः सततं कार्यं कर्म समाचर ।
असक्तो ह्याचरन्कर्म परमाप्नोति पूरुषः ॥ ३-१९ ॥

tasmād asaktaḥ satataṃ kāryaṃ karma samācara |
asakto hy ācaran karma param āpnoti pūruṣaḥ ||3-19||

Therefore, without being attached to the fruits of activities, one should act as a matter of duty. By working without attachment, one attains the Supreme.

श्रेयान्स्वधर्मो विगुणः परधर्मात्स्वनुष्ठितात् ।
स्वधर्मे निधनं श्रेयः परधर्मो भयावहः ॥ ३-३५ ॥

śreyān svadharmo viguṇaḥ paradharmāt svanuṣṭhitāt |
svadharme nidhanaṃ śreyaḥ paradharmo bhayāvahaḥ ||3-35||

It is far better to discharge one's own prescribed duties, even faultily, than another's duties, even perfectly. It is better to face death while performing one's own duties than engaging in someone else's duties. Following another's path is dangerous and fraught with fear.

Lord Krishna emphasizes the importance of following one's own duties diligently and to never try following someone else's path. For example, a spiritual leader needs to demonstrate non-violence and it is part of his duties. Even in the face of aggression, he is expected to be tolerant and non-violent. However, for a soldier at war, it is important to put down aggressive enemies using force. A soldier should not try to follow the spiritual master's non-violence in battle, and the spiritual master should never start shooting down his opponents. That is the moral of this shloka.

The law of karma is very complex and subjective. What is right for one person could be wrong for another. So it's very important for us to first understand what our duties are because that forms the basis for what is rightful action for us. Once we know what the rightful actions are for us, it is easier to avoid indulging in actions that would be considered inappropriate or sinful.

Arjuna then asks Lord Krishna, " what makes one compelled to engage in sinful acts unwillingly as if engaged by force?".

To this, Lord Krishna replies that " it is lust only which is the root cause".

As we have seen earlier, Lord Krishna has explained the lust aspect in detail in shlokas 2.62 & 2.63.

Many scholars have explained that lust & wrath can be transformed into friends by engaging them in the service of the Lord. For example, Shri [17]Hanuman [18]used his wrath to burn the city of Lanka. However, as he was doing this out of devotion to Lord Rama, he was considered the dearest devotee and this wrath was not considered sinful.

धूमेनाव्रियते वह्निर्यथादर्शो मलेन च ।
यथोल्बेनावृतो गर्भस्तथा तेनेदमावृतम् ॥ ३-३८ ॥

dhūmenāvriyate vahnir yathādarśo malena ca ।
yatholbenāvṛto garbhas tathā tenedam āvṛtam ॥3-38॥

As fire is covered by smoke, as a mirror is covered by dust, as the embryo is covered by the womb, our Consciousness is covered by different degrees of lust.

---

17 The term Sri or Shri mean the same thing and can be used interchangeably. It is a way of addressing respectful people.

18 The valorous monkey God from the epic Ramayana

इन्द्रियाणि मनो बुद्धिरस्याधिष्ठानमुच्यते ।
एतैर्विमोहयत्येष ज्ञानमावृत्य देहिनम् ॥ ३-४० ॥

indriyāṇi mano buddhir asyādhiṣṭhānam ucyate |
etair vimohayaty eṣa jñānam āvṛtya dehinam ||3-40||

The senses, the mind, and intelligence are the sitting places of this lust. Through them, lust covers the real knowledge of the living entity and bewilders him.

Lord Krishna provides wonderful analogies here to explain how lust could end up covering our entire consciousness.

तस्मात्त्वमिन्द्रियाण्यादौ नियम्य भरतर्षभ ।
पाप्मानं प्रजहिह्येनं ज्ञानविज्ञाननाशनम् ॥ ३-४१ ॥

tasmāt tvam indriyāṇy ādau niyamya bharatarṣabha |
pāpmānaṃ prajahihy enaṃ jñānavijñānanāśanam ||3-41||

Therefore, O best of the Bharatas, restrain and regulate your senses first, strike down this evil of lust, and slay this destroyer of self-realization and knowledge.

Commandment 5:

Know that lust is the root cause of all evil. Replace it with divine love for God.

CHAPTER 4

The Importance Of Commandments

यदा यदा हि धर्मस्य ग्लानिर्भवति भारत ।
अभ्युत्थानमधर्मस्य तदात्मानं सृजाम्यहम् ॥४-७॥

yadā yadā hi dharmasya glānir bhavati bhārata |
abhyutthānam adharmasya tadātmānaṃ sṛjāmy aham ||4-7||

Whenever there is a decline in dharma[19]*, and a rise in adharma (opposite of dharma), at that time, I manifest myself and descend on Earth.*

परित्राणाय साधूनां विनाशाय च दुष्कृताम् ।
धर्मसंस्थापनार्थाय संभवामि युगे युगे ॥४-८॥

paritrāṇāya sādhūnāṃ vināśāya ca duṣkṛtām |
dharmasaṃsthāpanārthāya saṃbhavāmi yuge yuge ||4-8||

For the protection of the virtuous, for the destruction of the wicked and for the establishment of dharma, I come into being in every age.

---

19 Dharma signifies both, the way of life as well as the law of life.

These two verses are comforting as well as disturbing. It is disturbing because the Lord says that the world will keep falling into disarray and there will be a chaotic descent into adharma, where the virtuous will suffer. The comforting part is that the Lord promises He will descend on earth and manifest himself every time this happens.

In my humble opinion, the thing to learn here is that humans have a general tendency to fall and become non-virtuous. So it is very important to consciously work on our own growth, have a connection with the Lord, follow his commandments and liberate ourselves.

This is one of the main motivations for why I set out on this journey to extract and document Lord Krishna's commandments.

काङ्क्षन्तः कर्मणां सिद्धिं यजन्त इह देवताः ।
क्षिप्रं हि मानुषे लोके सिद्धिर्भवति कर्मजा ॥४-१२॥

kāṅkṣantaḥ karmaṇāṃ siddhiṃ yajanta iha devatāḥ I
kṣipraṃ hi mānuṣe loke siddhir bhavati karmajā II4-12II

Hankering for success resulting from action in this world, people worship the Gods; Because success resulting from action is quickly attained in the human world.

Lord Krishna doesn't condemn any deity or the worshiping of any deities. However, He urges us to realize that there is only one ultimate Supreme God and that we should worship Him out of love rather than worshiping some deities for the sake of short term benefits.

Commandment 6

Worship the Supreme God and worship solely out of love, never to gain something.

तस्मादज्ञानसंभूतं हृत्स्थं ज्ञानासिनात्मनः ।
छित्त्वैनं संशयं योगमातिष्ठोत्तिष्ठ भारत ॥४-४२॥

tasmād ajñānasambhūtaṃ hṛtsthaṃ jñānāsinātmanaḥ I
chittvainaṃ saṃśayaṃ yogam ātiṣṭhottiṣṭha bhārata ll4-42ll

Therefore, cutting with the sword of knowledge, this doubt about the self, born of ignorance, residing in your heart, resort to yoga and arise O Bharata!

Shri Krishna says that this doubt which is creeping into your heart, crippling your life and action, destroy that doubt. This is the message given to Arjuna who was in a depressed state of mind. It is a very important message apt for anyone who is having self-doubt and feeling depressed.

As long as you suffer from self-doubt, you cannot attain higher consciousness or establish a connection with the divine Lord. Self-doubt is a stumbling block that prevents you from achieving any kind of success, either material or spiritual. So this has to be dealt with very firmly.

Swami Vivekananda explains these words of Lord Krishna very effectively by quoting this verse from Katha Upanishad: *"Destroy self-doubt with your intellect. Arise, awake and stop not until the goal is reached."*

Commandment 7

Destroy self-doubt. Your conviction in God depends upon your conviction in yourself.

CHAPTER 5

Four Paths, Six Obstacles, One Goal

यत्सांख्यैः प्राप्यते स्थानं तद्योगैरपि गम्यते ।
एकं सांख्यं च योगं च यः पश्यति स पश्यति ॥५-५॥

yat sāṃkhyaiḥ prāpyate sthānaṃ tad yogair api gamyate I
ekaṃ sāṃkhyaṃ ca yogaṃ ca yaḥ paśyati sa paśyati II5-5II

The goal that is reached by Samkhya[20] *(knowledge and analytical study) can also be attained by yoga. One who sees knowledge and yoga as one, alone sees.*

This is one such shloka where different scholars have introduced different interpretations of the word 'yoga'. Swami Prabhupada interprets this as "bhakti yoga (yoga of devotional service)". Swami Ranganathananda interprets this as "karma yoga (yoga of selfless action)", while Georg Feuerstein sticks to the literal interpretation of it being just yoga.

---

20 Samkhya, (Sanskrit: "Enumeration" or "Number") also spelled Sankhya, one of the six systems (darshans) of Indian philosophy. Samkhya adopts a consistent dualism of matter (prakriti) and the eternal spirit (purusha).

As laid out by Patanjali, the founding father of yoga, there are four major paths of yoga:

- Jnana yoga (yoga of knowledge and wisdom)
- Bhakti yoga (yoga of devotional service and divine love)
- Karma yoga (yoga of selfless action)
- Raja yoga (yoga of physical and mental control)

Many great sages and seers have repeatedly said that all four paths lead to the same ultimate goal of self-realization, union with the Supreme and ultimate liberation.

This is such a wonderful concept that shows that we humans have so much freedom to choose which path we want to take to reach God. Every person has a certain mental disposition and physical make up, based on which he/she can choose a combination of one or more of these paths.

Lord Krishna affirms this in this verse by saying that only those who can see these as one alone sees.

Success in any yoga is possible only by discipline, commitment, and consistency. And having control over our senses is absolutely critical without which success is not possible.

In this context, Swami Ranganathananda refers us to an insightful verse from the Hitopadesha[21] that says:

"Even in the forest, if one has sensory cravings, he or she will have trouble to lead a spiritual life; people with sensory attachments will face evil problems even when they go to the forest to live there in meditation. But, remaining at home with disciplined sense organs is real penance. Then, those who are engaged in blameless deeds, those who are free from sensory attachments, his or her own home becomes a forest retreat."

The primary emphasis is not on 'what you do' but rather on 'how you do it'. What you do (going to a mountain and meditating inside

21 Hitopadesha is an ancient India text comprising of many stories and fables with the goal of imparting wisdom to the masses.

a cave) is futile if you are failing in the 'how' part by not having control over your senses.

There are many negative qualities of our senses which Lord Krishna explains in detail in later chapters. However, there are at least six major obstacles/defects (vikaras[22]) that we are all born with which we should strive to overcome. They are kama (lust), krodha (anger), moha (attachment), lobha (greed), matsarya (jealousy) and ahankar (arrogance, ego). It is our duty to control and overcome these in order to achieve spiritual success.

Victory over these requires discipline, humility, and focus. Just like you have to eat every day and sleep every day, you have to keep working on overcoming these defects every day. If you are careless for even one day, these can always creep back into your mind.

शक्नोतीहैव यः सोढुं प्राक्शरीरविमोक्षणात् ।
कामक्रोधोद्भवं वेगं स युक्तः स सुखी नरः ॥५-२३॥

śaknotīhaiva yaḥ soḍhuṃ prāk śarīravimokṣaṇāt ।
kāmakrodhodbhavaṃ vegaṃ sa yuktaḥ sa sukhī naraḥ ॥5-23॥

In this human form, whoever is able to withstand the tremendous current arising from lust and anger will be a yogi and a happy being.

Lord Krishna clearly calls out kama (lust) and krodha (anger) as the top two problems or vikaras that we have to absolutely control and overcome. He tells us that these are very strong and powerful forces and whoever succeeds in overcoming these would be called a yogi.

Commandment 8:

Be committed and consistent with yoga. Vanquish your vikaras. You will find God then.

---

22 There are six major sensory defects which are termed as vikaras

CHAPTER 6

Yoga Of The Self, By The Self, For The Self

अनाश्रितः कर्मफलं कार्यं कर्म करोति यः ।
स संन्यासी च योगी च न निरग्निर्न चाक्रियः ॥ ६-१ ॥

anāśritaḥ karmaphalaṃ kāryaṃ karma karoti yaḥ |
sa saṃnyāsī ca yogī ca na niragnir na cākriyaḥ ||6-1||

One who performs one's duties and rightful actions without depending upon the fruit of action, is a true sannyasi (renouncer) and of steadfast mind. Not the one who does not handle fire nor the one who performs no action.

The term "the one who does not handle fire", refers to renounced beings who depend on alms for their living and do not cook their own food.

Lord Krishna reiterates that the best path towards liberation and spiritual growth lies in action without expectation and not in inaction.

Georg Feuerstein beautifully summarizes this as follows:

> "This stanza epitomizes the ideal of inner or symbolic renunciation. i.e, renunciation IN action rather than renunciation OF action."

Desire leads to urge, which leads to action. The root cause of all action is desire. Desires arise out of our wants. We need to differentiate between needs and wants. Needs have to be fulfilled. Wants can never be fulfilled. Wants are endless.

That is a very insightful verse in the Srimad Bhagavatham[23]. 9.19.14.

"Na jatu kamah kaamanam upbhogena sanyati" which means "desire is not quenched by satisfying the desire. It only gets inflamed like fire in which butter is poured."

Most of us feel that once we satisfy our desires, we can become desireless. However, that's the game of maya. That's the trap you should avoid. **Desires only get stronger when fulfilled**.

उद्धरेदात्मनात्मानं नात्मानमवसादयेत् ।
आत्मैव ह्यात्मनो बन्धुरात्मैव रिपुरात्मनः ॥६-५॥

uddhared ātmanātmānaṃ nātmānam avasādayet ।
ātmaiva hy ātmano bandhur ātmaiva ripur ātmanaḥ ॥6-5॥

You should raise Yourself by yourself. You should not let yourself bring your self down. For you alone are your own friend. You alone are your own enemy.

This is such a profound and impactful message! That we are responsible for ourselves. That we are empowered to make ourselves successful. We do not need to depend on any external factors for our success nor should we hold anyone else accountable for our

23 Srimad Bhagavatham is one of the most important classics of India describing the life and times of Lord Krishna

failures. Our own inner self holds the key to ultimate success and realization of God.

The Sufi poet Rumi[24] has said this beautifully:

Man arafa nai sahu
Faqo araba nab bahu

He alone who recognizes his own self can recognize God.

Rumi also says this:

"In each human spirit is a Christ concealed,
to be helped or hindered, to be hurt or healed.
If from any human soul you lift the veil,
you will find a Christ there without fail."

बन्धुरात्मात्मनस्तस्य येनात्मैवात्मना जितः ।
अनात्मनस्तु शत्रुत्वे वर्तेतात्मैव शत्रुवत् ॥ ६-६ ॥

bandhur ātmātmanas tasya yenātmaivātmanā jitaḥ ।
anātmanas tu śatrutve vartetātmaiva śatruvat ॥6-6॥

Lord Krishna says that "*for him who has conquered the mind, the mind is the best of friends, and for one who has failed to do so, the mind will remain the greatest enemy.*"

Our higher self is our spirit soul and our lower self is our mind. It is a profoundly beautiful concept of the self being the friend or enemy of the self. The self, keeping a watch on the self, and the self, helping with the liberation of the self.

If we can understand this fully, we can get closer to understanding God and His divine design. Good and evil are both different aspects of the self and the goal is for the good self to achieve victory over the evil self.

---

24 Jalaluddin Rumi was a 13th-century Persian poet and Sufi mystic

नात्यश्नतस्तु योगो ऽस्ति न चैकान्तमनश्नतः ।
न चातिस्वप्नशीलस्य जाग्रतो नैव चार्जुन ॥६-१६॥

nātyaśnatas tu yogo 'sti na caikāntam anaśnataḥ I
na cātisvapnaśīlasya jāgrato naiva cārjuna II6-16II

Success in yoga is not for the person who eats too much or does not eat anything at all. Nor for one who sleeps too much or does not sleep at all.

युक्ताहारविहारस्य युक्तचेष्टस्य कर्मसु ।
युक्तस्वप्नावबोधस्य योगो भवति दुःखहा ॥६-१७॥

yuktāhāravihārasya yuktaceṣṭasya karmasu I
yuktasvapnāvabodhasya yogo bhavati duḥkhahā II6-17II

Yoga will help dispel all sufferings of the one who is moderate, balanced and regulated in his habits of eating, sleeping, working and recreation.

Commandment 9

Control the mind by practicing moderation in eating, sleeping, working, and recreation.

CHAPTER 7
Knowing Maya

As mentioned in shloka 3.38, there are many layers of lust and 'maya[25]' that covers our intellect and consciousness. It is this maya that makes it so hard for us to realize God.

The Rig Veda[26] and other ancient scriptures including some Hebrew and Aramaic ones all say that 'there are many names and many forms but the absolute truth is one and the same'.

मनुष्याणां सहस्रेषु कश्चिद्यतति सिद्धये ।
यततामपि सिद्धानां कश्चिन्मां वेत्ति तत्त्वतः ॥७-३॥

manuṣyāṇāṃ sahasreṣu kaś cid yatati siddhaye |
yatatām api siddhānāṃ kaś cin māṃ vetti tattvataḥ ||7-3||

Among thousands of people, only a handful really strive for spiritual perfection. Even among those, just a few understand Me as I truly am.

Lord Krishna gives an idea of how small the success rate is among humans when it comes to realizing God. Why is it so? What is the

25 Maya is an umbrella term used for all types of ignorance, illusions and delusions our mind is subjected to

26 The Rigveda is an ancient Indian collection of Vedic Sanskrit hymns believed to be passed on by God Himself

biggest cause of impediment? It is very important for us to know and understand this.

The ancient Chinese philosopher Sun Tzu has said this very effectively in his book the 'Art of war'.

"If you know the enemy and know yourself, you need not fear the result of a hundred battles. If you know yourself but not the enemy, for every victory gained you will also suffer a defeat. If you know neither the enemy nor yourself, you will succumb in every battle."

In the sixth chapter, especially in verse 6.5, Shri Krishna urges us to know our self. In this chapter, He urges us to know the enemy (maya). This combined knowledge is what is going to assure us success in our battle of life.

All our vikaras that we discussed in chapter 5 arise out of this maya. And as described in chapter 1, the most important first step for us is to identify and catch this enemy using our intellect.

ये चैव सात्त्विका भावा राजसास्तामसाश्च ये ।
मत्त एवेति तान्विद्धि न त्वहं तेषु ते मयि ॥७-१२॥

ye caiva sāttvikā bhāvā rājasās tāmasāś ca ye ।
matta eveti tān viddhi na tv ahaṃ teṣu te mayi ॥7-12॥

And whatever states pertaining to sattva (goodness, constructive, harmonious) and those pertaining to rajas (based on passion, tendency to be confusing) and to tamas (badness, darkness, ignorance, destructive, chaotic) are there, know them to proceed from Me alone. Yet I am not bound by them.

Lord Krishna says that all the qualities good and bad originate from the same Supreme Lord, however, He is not bound by them. If you peek inside yourself, you will find that both good and bad exists inside you. The goal of life is to use your intellect to make sure that the good in you always wins over the bad in you.

दैवी ह्येषा गुणमयी मम माया दुरत्यया ।
मामेव ये प्रपद्यन्ते मायामेतां तरन्ति ते ॥७-१४॥

daivī hy eṣā guṇamayī mama māyā duratyayā I
mām eva ye prapadyante māyām etāṃ taranti te II7-14II

Verily, this maya of mine constituted of the gunas [27] (three qualities) is difficult to cross over. Those who devote themselves to Me alone, cross over this illusion.

Maya has two dimensions: 'vidya maya' and 'avidya maya'. Vidya maya is the maya of knowledge. The good maya. While avidya maya is the maya of ignorance, the bad maya. Both good and bad are aspects of the same maya. It is our goal and duty to strengthen the vidya maya and eradicate or control the avidya maya in us. The ability to do this is the single biggest differentiator between humans and all other life forms.

The point to note is that good is also maya but we have to use it to overcome bad which is again maya. **Thus, we should fight maya with maya.**

That's a hint about the grand design of the Lord Supreme. Use yourself to raise yourself. Use maya to fight and win over maya.

Here again, saint Kabir mentions this very effectively in two lines:

माया है दो प्रकार की, जो कोइ जाने खाय |
एक मिलावे राम को, एक नरक ले जाय ||

Maya hai do prakar ki, jo koi jane khay.

Ek milave Ram ko, ek narak le jaay.

Maya has two forms. A rare one knows of them. One leads you to the beloved Lord while the other leads you to hell.

---

27 Vedic literature classifies everything as consisting of three gunas – Sattvic(goodness), Rajasic (passion) and Tamasic(badness, ignorance)

But this is easier said than done. The first step in our battle is to know the enemy and understand how to win over it. However, actual victory is possible only when we attain the grace of the Lord. It is the benevolence of God alone that can help us gain the ultimate victory.

Sri Ramakrishna Paramahansa explains the difference between attachment and compassion (maya and daya) in his famous works 'Vedanta Kesari' thus.

"Remember that daya (compassion) and maya (attachment), are two different things. Attachment means the feeling of 'my-ness' towards one's relatives.

Compassion is the love one feels for all beings of the world. It is an attitude of equality. Maya also comes from God. Through maya, God makes one serve one's relatives. But one thing should be remembered. Maya keeps us in ignorance and entangles us in the world, whereas daya makes our hearts pure and gradually unties our bonds."

CHAPTER 8
The Importance Of Habit And Consistency

अन्तकाले च मामेव स्मरन्मुक्त्वा कलेवरम् ।
यः प्रयाति स मद्भावं याति नास्त्यत्र संशयः ॥८-५॥

antakāle ca mām eva smaran muktvā kalevaram ।
yaḥ prayāti sa madbhāvaṃ yāti nāsty atra saṃśayaḥ ॥8-5॥

A person who thinks of Me and meditates upon Me at the time of death attains Me after leaving the body. There is no doubt about this.

The last moments of one's life is called 'antakale'. Here, Lord Krishna is promising that whoever thinks of Him and meditates upon Him during his last moments, will definitely reach Him.

I used to attend Gita sessions. My younger son who was 8 years old at that time, used to accompany me often. When this particular shloka was discussed, he seemed a bit doubtful and disturbed. Upon questioning, he mentioned that he could not comprehend this particular promise of God. He said "are you saying that people can do all bad things in their lives and just have to think of God at the time of death and they just reach God? This doesn't seem fair to all the good people who are always being good boys in their lives".

He had this look in his eyes that seemed to ask "why do you ask me to be a good boy all the time? I can just think of Lord Krishna at the time of my death and then I will become all good".

What a wonderful question indeed. I told him to have a little bit of patience because Lord Krishna is explaining that very thing in the next shloka ☺. The fact is that, during one's last moments, a person can only think of things that he has been attached to in his life. A miser will think of money, a hunter may think of some animal, a politician may think of power, etc.

Swami Prabhupada gives the example of the great king Bharata. Although he was wise and an ethical king, he thought of a deer during his death and accordingly attained the body of a deer during his next birth.

यं यं वापि स्मरन्भावं त्यजत्यन्ते कलेवरम् ।
तं तमेवैति कौन्तेय सदा तद्भावभावितः ॥८-६॥

yaṃ yaṃ vāpi smaran bhāvaṃ tyajaty ante kalevaram |
taṃ tam evaiti kaunteya sadā tadbhāvabhāvitaḥ ||8-6||

Remembering at the end of life, whatever divine form or object, that alone is reached by that person, because of one's constant thought of that object in his/her life.

अनन्यचेताः सततं यो मां स्मरति नित्यशः ।
तस्याहं सुलभः पार्थ नित्ययुक्तस्य योगिनः ॥८-१४॥

ananyacetāḥ satataṃ yo māṃ smarati nityaśaḥ |
tasyāhaṃ sulabhaḥ pārtha nityayuktasya yoginaḥ ||8-14||

For one who always remembers me without deviation and is constantly engaged in devotional service, I am easy to attain.

Thus, only a person of good nature, with humility and who has practiced devotion to God and lead a good life can actually think of God during his/her last moments. There is no cheating possible here.

Lord Krishna's assurance should actually inspire us to lead a good life so that we may be able to think of Him during our last moments and attain liberation.

The requirement of consistency and habit of practicing devotion and humility is extremely important. Without this, we cannot achieve any success on the spiritual path (or any path for that matter). There are some Christian texts which say the same thing as 'It is largely through "habits of holiness" that the Spirit transforms us'.

This explanation seemed agreeable to my little boy and he promised to take efforts to remain a good boy all his life. All Glory to Krishna!

CHAPTER 9

The Assurance Of God

इदं तु ते गुह्यतमं प्रवक्ष्याम्यनसूयवे ।
ज्ञानं विज्ञानसहितं यज्ज्ञात्वा मोक्ष्यसे ऽशुभात् ॥९-१॥

idaṃ tu te guhyatamaṃ pravakṣyāmy anasūyave I
jñānaṃ vijñānasahitaṃ yaj jñātvā mokṣyase 'śubhāt II9-1II

Here, I am going to tell you the profound truth, because your mind is free from jealousy. I shall impart to you this most confidential knowledge and realization, knowing which, you shall be relieved of the miseries of material existence.

राजविद्या राजगुह्यं पवित्रमिदमुत्तमम् ।
प्रत्यक्षावगमं धर्म्यं सुसुखं कर्तुमव्ययम् ॥९-२॥

rājavidyā rājaguhyaṃ pavitram idam uttamam I
pratyakṣāvagamaṃ dharmyaṃ susukhaṃ kartum avyayam II9-2II

This knowledge is the king of all knowledge, the most secret of all secrets. It is the purest knowledge, and because it gives the direct perception of the self by realization, it is the perfection of religion. It is everlasting, and it is joyfully performed.

A very important message and assurance that Shri Krishna conveys in this verse is through the word 'pratyaksavagamam', which means 'which can be realized by direct experience'. This is an assurance that God can be a constant awareness in our day to day life and He is our innermost self.

On similar lines, Shri Krishna has provided further context in the 24th verse of chapter 4.

ब्रह्मार्पणं ब्रह्महविर्ब्रह्माग्नौ ब्रह्मणा हुतम् ।
ब्रह्मैव तेन गन्तव्यं ब्रह्मकर्मसमाधिना ॥४-२४॥

brahmārpaṇaṃ brahmahavir brahmāgnau brahmaṇā hutam ।
brahmaiva tena gantavyaṃ brahmakarmasamādhinā ॥4-24॥

The offering is Brahman [28]*. The one who offers is Brahman. The fire is Brahman. The result is Brahman. Everything is Brahman.*

This is the ultimate and universal truth. Everything we see around us is essentially the same infinite, pure, absolute consciousness manifested in various forms.

To realize this and achieve the experience of this divine consciousness in everything and everyone is the purpose of this human life. It helps to reaffirm yourself constantly that the Supreme God is the seed and source of all that exists in the universe.

Consistent practice of devotion not only helps at the time of death but also during our current life as well. Here is a very kind and reassuring promise by the Lord.

अनन्याश्चिन्तयन्तो मां ये जनाः पर्युपासते ।
तेषां नित्याभियुक्तानां योगक्षेमं वहाम्यहम् ॥९-२२॥

ananyāś cintayanto māṃ ye janāḥ paryupāsate ।
teṣāṃ nityābhiyuktānāṃ yogakṣemaṃ vahāmy aham ॥9-22॥

28 Brahman is the Sanskrit term for the Supreme consciousness or Supreme God.

Those who think of Me and nothing else, those who worship Me with one-pointed mind, to them, who are constantly in a spirit of yoga, I provide what they lack and preserve what they have.

It is so reassuring. **I provide what they lack and preserve what they have.**

Following His 10th commandment will help you gain His protection in this material world as well as the afterlife.

Commandment 10

Seeing God in everything and everyone, practice devotion and humility consistently.

Many of us have many regrets and live in guilt. We many times wonder if we can ever be deserving of God's love. Shri Krishna's next message is very encouraging and reassuring to all of us.

अपि चेत्सुदुराचारो भजते मामनन्यभाक् ।
साधुरेव स मन्तव्यः सम्यग्व्यवसितो हि सः ॥९-३०॥

api cet sudurācāro bhajate mām ananyabhāk |
sādhur eva sa mantavyaḥ samyag vyavasito hi saḥ ||9-30||

If even a wicked person worships Me, with one-pointed devotion, he or she should be regarded as good, for he or she has very rightly resolved.

We will be forgiven. Our past will be resolved. A new life will commence.

That's the power of bhakti (devotion).

CHAPTER 10
Glimpses Of The Divine

यो मामजमनादिं च वेत्ति लोकमहेश्वरम् ।
असंमूढः स मर्त्येषु सर्वपापैः प्रमुच्यते ॥ १०-३ ॥

yo mām ajam anādiṃ ca vetti lokamaheśvaram ।
asaṃmūḍhaḥ sa martyeṣu sarvapāpaiḥ pramucyate ॥10-3॥

He who knows Me as unborn and beginning-less, as the great Lord of the worlds, he, among mortals, is undeluded and he is liberated from all sins.

The gist of this verse is that the very act of realizing the Supreme Lord's unbounded nature is sufficient to purify a person completely and liberate him from the clutches of maya.

तेषां सततयुक्तानां भजतां प्रीतिपूर्वकम् ।
ददामि बुद्धियोगं तं येन मामुपयान्ति ते ॥ १०-१० ॥

teṣāṃ satatayuktānāṃ bhajatāṃ prītipūrvakam ।
dadāmi buddhiyogaṃ taṃ yena mām upayānti te ॥10-10॥

To them who are ever steadfast, worshiping Me with love, I grant that 'buddhi[29]*yoga' or devotional attitude of a mature state by which they can reach Me.*

This is another beautiful and strong message from the Lord for those who are consistent, committed and unwavering in their devotion.

'Buddhi-yoga' is the wisdom and positive thought force that will help us to reach or attain God. It is said in the Mahabharata that when the Demi-Gods want to destroy a person, they just turn away his/her buddhi (intellect) in a bad direction. Then that person will destroy himself/herself.

One of Chanakya's [30] famous quotes is "*Vinasa kale vipareet buddhi*", which means "intelligence leaves the man at the time when destruction is imminent".

Lord Krishna is telling us that He will do the opposite, wherein, He will help turn our buddhi in a good direction that will help us liberate ourselves and attain Him.

The beauty of this verse lies in the fact that the Lord is implying that **He is going to help us and not force us.** So, ultimately we are accountable and empowered to go in either direction, positive or negative, based on how we use our buddhi. I suppose this is what is termed as 'free will' in many western texts.

The famous Greek philosopher Socrates had a very compelling and strong view about free will which resonates with the messages of the Bhagavad Gita.

As per Socrates' view, free will is impossible without self-control. For people without self-control are not capable of free will because they are themselves slaves to their passions and ignorance. If they

---

29 Buddhi means intellect

30 Chanakya was an Indian philosopher, economist, jurist and royal advisor. He authored the ancient Indian political treatise, the Arthashastra.

had the free will, they would have gained victory and control over themselves.

What a deep thought! The general society looks at free will only as what you can or cannot do 'externally'. You can go to any place you want, wear any clothes you want and so on. However, **the true free will is the will to have mastery over yourself**. In the external facing world, slaves cannot be called as 'free' as they live under bondage to their masters. Similarly, in the bigger, internal world, we cannot claim to be free or as having free will as long as we remain slaves to our own senses and ignorance.

Lord Krishna says that He will provide us with the required intellect to see this so that we can actually learn to use our free will in the right direction and attain true freedom and liberation. When we say we have to 'reach God', it is not an alien destination. God is inside each one of us as expounded by Lord Krishna in previous verses, especially verse 3.38 which makes it clear that what is required for us is to use our intellect to destroy the layers of dust and ignorance that covers our inner self. Once we manage to do that, we would have reached God because by definition, the moment you realize God (the self within), you attain Him.

The whole of the 10th chapter describes the manifested glory of the Lord and provides a strong base on which you can place the 10th commandment and follow it.

In my humble opinion, **the 10th commandment can help us follow all the other commandments**. These commandments lead us towards liberation from this endless cycle of birth and death in this material world.

CHAPTER 11

The Omnipresence And Opulence Of God

In the ancient Sanskrit texts, this chapter is termed as the 'viswarupa darshanam', meaning 'the vision of the Universal form'. Here, Lord Krishna helps Arjuna actually see and realize the omnipresence and opulence of the Lord. He wants Arjuna to see and understand how He is everywhere and in everything.

मत्कर्मकृन्मत्परमो मद्भक्तः सङ्गवर्जितः ।
निर्वैरः सर्वभूतेषु यः स मामेति पाण्डव ॥ ११-५५ ॥

matkarmakṛn matparamo madbhaktaḥ saṅgavarjitaḥ I
nirvairaḥ sarvabhūteṣu yaḥ sa mām eti pāṇḍava ||11-55||

This one verse summarizes what you need to do to succeed in reaching God.

'matkarmakrn'	**→ Devoting your actions (karma) to God. May your actions always be to serve Him.**
'matparamo'	**→ Considering Me as the supreme goal.**
'madbhaktah'	**→ Always devoted to Me (devoting your mind to God).**
'sangavarjitah'	**→ Free from sensory attachments.**
'nirvairah sarvabhutesu'	**→ Without enmity or hatred towards all living beings.**
'yah'	**→ One who is such.**
'sa mam eti'	**→ He comes unto Me (he attains Me).**

As per Sankaracharya[31], this verse contains the gist of the entire Gita which is capable of taking us to the highest planes and liberation. This is what one has to practice and live by.

Point to be noted is that 'detachment' does not mean 'apathy'. It does not mean that you do not care.

Swami Ranganathananda explains the term 'detachment' very beautifully during one of his essays and it goes like this: suppose you have a child and you love him/her. Now, if you are detached, you will be able to love your neighbor's child also the same way you love your own child. Attachment causes 'me and mine'. Detachment focuses on the love. The same kind of unconditional love that God has for all beings.

This is such an important concept. **Detachment actually helps your love grow and become all-encompassing.**

When you are in a state of complete detachment, you will automatically be in a state of absolute and unconditional love. A state where you will actually realize the Lord's presence in every being and be devoid of hatred towards any living being. Later on, in the

---

31 Sankaracharya, also known as 'Adi Sankaracharya' was an 8th century Indian philosopher & saint. He is considered to be one of the foremost proponent of the philosophy of Advaita (non-dualistic nature of God).

13th chapter, Lord Krishna gives a scientific explanation regarding his omnipresence.

Commandment 11:

Be compassionate and do not have hatred towards any living being.

CHAPTER 12
The Path Of Bhakti (Devotion)

There are two fundamental aspects of God. One is the manifested, personal form and the other is the un-manifested, impersonal, imperishable, formless nature.

In very broad terms, jnana yoga deals with the non-personal aspect of God, while bhakti yoga deals with His personal, manifested aspect. Both ultimately lead to the same glorious goal as confirmed by Shri Krishna in verse 5.5 explained in chapter 5.

This chapter deals primarily with bhakti yoga. It starts with Arjuna asking Shri Krishna "what is better, the path of bhakti for the manifested form or the path of jnana for the un-manifested aspect of God?".

Lord Krishna responds that bhakti is better although both reach the same destination.

क्लेशो ऽधिकतरस्तेषामव्यक्तासक्तचेतसाम् ।
अव्यक्ता हि गतिर्दुःखं देहवद्भिरवाप्यते ॥ १२-५ ॥

kleśo 'dhikataras teṣām avyaktāsaktacetasām ।
avyaktā hi gatir duḥkhaṃ dehavadbhir avāpyate ॥12-5॥

Greater is their trouble whose minds are set on the un-manifested. For the goal of the un-manifested is very hard to be reached by the manifested souls (embodied persons).

So, Shri Krishna says that the path of jnana is very difficult for those with body-consciousness (aware of your body). Whereas, the path of bhakti is meant for all.

मय्येव मन आधत्स्व मयि बुद्धिं निवेशय ।
निवसिष्यसि मय्येव अत ऊर्ध्वं न संशयः ॥१२-८॥

mayy eva mana ādhatsva mayi buddhiṃ niveśaya ।
nivasiṣyasi mayy eva ata ūrdhvaṃ na saṃśayaḥ ॥12-8॥

Just fix your mind upon God. Engage your wisdom faculty (buddhi) on God. Then, without a doubt, you will always live in God hereafter.

As discussed earlier, Lord Krishna has already explained that He is the manifestation of the Supreme God. So, wherever He uses the term 'Me', you can replace it with 'God' without it changing the meaning of the verse. Especially when Lord Krishna Himself explains the un-manifested aspect of God where there is no 'Me'.

अथ चित्तं समाधातुं न शक्नोषि मयि स्थिरम् ।
अभ्यासयोगेन ततो मामिच्छाप्तुं धनंजय ॥१२-९॥

atha cittaṃ samādhātuṃ na śaknoṣi mayi sthiram ।
abhyāsayogena tato mām icchāptuṃ dhanaṃjaya ॥12-9॥

If you are unable to fix your mind steadily on God, then by 'abhyasa yoga' seek to reach God.

'Abhyasa yoga' literally means the 'yoga of practice'. Some scholars have interpreted this to mean following a disciplined regimen and practicing bhakti yoga regularly until you are able to achieve the one-pointed devotion to the Lord.

अभ्यासे ऽप्यसमर्थो ऽसि मत्कर्मपरमो भव ।
मदर्थमपि कर्माणि कुर्वन्सिद्धिमवाप्स्यसि ॥१२-१०॥

abhyāse 'py asamartho 'si matkarmaparamo bhava I
madartham api karmāṇi kurvan siddhim avāpsyasi ||12-10||

If you are unable to follow even abhyasa yoga, then just make sure all your actions are dedicated to God. Even by doing actions for the sake of God, you shall attain perfection.

Remember verse 11.55 and the 11th commandment. Dedicate all your actions to the Lord. If you are a good singer, sing for the Lord. If you are a good dancer, dance for the Lord. If you are a good cook, cook for the Lord. Whatever you enjoy doing, do it and dedicate it to the Lord.

There is a story in the 'vana parva' section of the Mahabaratha about a butcher who becomes enlightened. Although his profession entails him to killing innocent animals and selling them for money, because he was always performing his duty without attachment and was always dedicating his work to the Lord, he becomes enlightened. He even plays the role of a teacher for the learned and virtuous Pandavas. The moral of this story is that no work is lowly or lofty, it is the way you perform your work that makes it worthy or unworthy. And any work performed without attachment and dedicated to the Lord will only make you eligible for enlightenment.

There is an important distinction I would like to make here. This story in no way absolves you from the sin of killing other living beings. What we should remember is that in older days, every person was tied to a specific profession based on which family they are born into. If you were born into a family of butchers, you had to become a butcher yourself. In those circumstances, the best you could do was to do your duty without attachment and by dedicating it to the Lord.

In today's world, we do not have any such restrictions. We all have a freedom to choose what we want to do as a profession. Killing any creature should never be out of choice especially if there was no compelling reason for you to do so.

Remember shloka 3.35 where the Lord stresses the importance of following one's own dharma and doing one's own duties.

And remember verse 2.47 where the Lord explains the importance of doing your duties without being attached to the fruits or results of your actions.

It all put together, provides the secret key to success in the spiritual plane.

अथैतदप्यशक्तो ऽसि कर्तुं मद्योगमाश्रितः ।
सर्वकर्मफलत्यागं ततः कुरु यतात्मवान् ॥ १२-११ ॥

athaitad apy aśakto 'si kartuṃ madyogam āśritaḥ ।
sarvakarmaphalatyāgaṃ tataḥ kuru yatātmavān ॥12-11॥

If you are unable to do even this, then, taking refuge in God, abandon the fruit of all actions, being self-controlled.

Lord Krishna has provided an incremental, **step-wise plan for success and liberation** based on the level of difficulty and the capabilities of each person. We can formulate it as follows:

Step 1: Stop expecting fruits or results of your actions (verse 12.11 & 2.47)
Step 2: Dedicate all your actions to the Lord. (verse 12.10)
Step 3: Follow a disciplined life and continuously practice devotion to the Lord (verse 12.9)
Step 4: Fix your mind on the Lord and engage all your intellect and wisdom upon Him. (12.8)
Step 5: You succeed! You will become dear to the Lord and get liberated.

CHAPTER 13

The Science Behind Spirituality

The 13th chapter of Bhagavad Gita is a very scientific analysis and study of various aspects of nature and the laws governing nature. This is a glimpse into jnana yoga and Samkhya philosophy.

In some versions of the Bhagavad Gita, including the ones by Bhaktivedanta Swami Prabhupada, this chapter is shown to start with a question by Arjuna who wants to know and learn about aspects like 'kshetra' and 'kshetrajna'. However, many other scholars including Sankaracharya, Swami Ranganathananda, and Georg Feuerstein don't think that Arjuna's question is part of the original manuscript and so they directly start with Krishna's address to Arjuna.

The only reason I am pointing this out here is that the numbering of the verses/shlokas in this chapter will be off by 1 depending on which version of the Gita you are referring to. For example, verse number 13.6 that we discuss here will actually be verse number 13.7 in Bhaktivedanta Swami Prabhupada's version of the Gita.

We start with the study of '**kshetra**' (field) and '**kshetrajna**' (knower of the field). Lord Krishna prods us to discriminate between the field and the knower of the field.

इदं शरीरं कौन्तेय क्षेत्रमित्यभिधीयते ।
एतद्यो वेत्ति तं प्राहुः क्षेत्रज्ञ इति तद्विदः ॥१३-१॥

idaṃ śarīraṃ kaunteya kṣetram ity abhidhīyate ।
etad yo vetti taṃ prāhuḥ kṣetrajña iti tadvidaḥ ॥13-1॥

This body, O Arjuna, is called the field; he who knows it is called the knower of the field, by those who know of them.

Everything in this universe that you can feel or perceive with your senses belongs to 'kshetra' or the 'field'. The infinite intelligence and the source of this observed universe is the 'kshetrajna' or 'knower of the field'.

Lord Krishna provides a detailed classification of the kshetra below.

महाभूतान्यहंकारो बुद्धिरव्यक्तमेव च ।
इन्द्रियाणि दशैकं च पञ्च चेन्द्रियगोचराः ॥१३-५॥

mahābhūtāny ahaṃkāro buddhir avyaktam eva ca ।
indriyāṇi daśaikaṃ ca pañca cendriyagocarāḥ ॥13-5॥

इच्छा द्वेषः सुखं दुःखं संघातश्चेतना धृतिः ।
एतत्क्षेत्रं समासेन सविकारमुदाहृतम् ॥१३-६॥

icchā dveṣaḥ sukhaṃ duḥkhaṃ saṃghātaś cetanā dhṛtiḥ ।
etat kṣetraṃ samāsena savikāram udāhṛtam ॥13-6॥

The great primordial elements (earth, water, fire, air and ether), egoism, intellect & the un-manifested stage of the three modes of nature, the ten senses (five perceptive senses – eyes, ears, nose, tongue & skin + five action senses – voice, legs, hands, anus & genitals), the one mind & the five objects of the senses (smell, taste, form, touch & sound), then desire, hatred, pleasure, pain, the aggregate (the body), intellect, conviction.

In all, these are the 24 categories to deal with in the universe and the 25th is 'Purusa[32]' which is the nature of pure consciousness.

Thus, Lord Krishna summarizes as:

etat kṣetraṃ samāsena savikāram udāhṛtam

I have illustrated this kshetra fully along with their modifications or interactions.

It is a good exercise for everyone to contemplate upon all these 24 kshetras, see if you are able to identify and understand each and how they relate to you as well as with each other. If you can do that, you would have made good progress in the area of 'jnana yoga'.

Lord Krishna then goes on to explain what is the knowledge that we should endeavor to seek (jnana).

अमानित्वमदम्भित्वमहिंसा क्षान्तिरार्जवम् ।
आचार्योपासनं शौचं स्थैर्यमात्मविनिग्रहः ॥ १३-७ ॥

amānitvam adambhitvam ahiṃsā kṣāntir ārjavam I
ācāryopāsanaṃ śaucaṃ sthairyam ātmavinigrahaḥ II13-7II

Mana (mind) is associated with 'I' and egoistic attitude. 'Amanitvam' is without this egoistic attitude and implies humility.

Shri Krishna starts classifying knowledge or jnana with humility being the first in the list. Without humility, we cannot gain any knowledge.

Then follows 'unpretentiousness, non-violence, moderation, righteousness, service to the teacher, purity, steadiness, and self-control'.

It must be noted that throughout the Gita, Shri Krishna has advised the practice of compassion, non-hatred and non-violence as very important virtues.

---

32 Purusa is the pure consciousness or infinite intelligence

Non-violence is a virtue and benefits you. It is very different from cowardice. Non-violence is when you are capable of violence but choose not to be violent. By choosing non-violence, you are avoiding bad karma and doing yourself a huge favor. Violence is acceptable only when it is used to prevent the other person from doing anything that is going to result in bad karma. Exactly what situations and actions qualify as bad karma is laid down in various treatises on 'dharma[33]'.

इन्द्रियार्थेषु वैराग्यमनहंकार एव च ।
जन्ममृत्युजराव्याधिदुःखदोषानुदर्शनम् ॥ १३-८ ॥

indriyārtheṣu vairāgyam anahaṃkāra eva ca ।
janmamṛtyujarāvyādhiduḥkhadoṣānudarśanam ॥13-8॥

Detachment from sensory objects, the absence of egoism or superiority complex, ability to constantly reflect upon the evils of birth, death, old age, sickness & pain.

असक्तिरनभिष्वङ्गः पुत्रदारगृहादिषु ।
नित्यं च समचित्तत्वमिष्टानिष्टोपपत्तिषु ॥ १३-९ ॥

asaktir anabhiṣvaṅgaḥ putradāragṛhādiṣu ।
nityaṃ ca samacittatvam iṣṭāniṣṭopapattiṣu ॥13-9॥

Spirit of detachment, not getting entangled or identifying the self, based on son, spouse, home, etc. Constant even-mindedness in the face of desirable as well as undesirable occurrences.

Remember commandment 2.

---

33 Dharma is a term used to define the laws of life, way of life and the principle of cosmic order.

मयि चानन्ययोगेन भक्तिरव्यभिचारिणी ।
विविक्तदेशसेवित्वमरतिर्जनसंसदि ॥ १३-१० ॥

mayi cānanyayogena bhaktir avyabhicāriṇī ।
viviktadeśasevitvam aratir janasaṃsadi ॥13-10॥

Unswerving devotion to Me via bhakti yoga, inclination to appreciate solitude, distaste for the constant company of men and women.

Creativity requires introspection and that requires solitude. You cannot be creative if you are always amidst a crowd of people.

अध्यात्मज्ञाननित्यत्वं तत्त्वज्ञानार्थदर्शनम् ।
एतज्ज्ञानमिति प्रोक्तमज्ञानं यदतो ऽन्यथा ॥ १३-११ ॥

adhyātmajñānanityatvaṃ tattvajñānārthadarśanam ।
etaj jñānam iti proktam ajñānaṃ yad ato 'nyathā ॥13-11॥

Constant application of spiritual knowledge, realizing the purpose of true knowledge, this is declared to be true knowledge and what is opposed to this is ignorance.

These are all that constitutes as knowledge or 'jnana' according to Krishna.

Just as there is a kshetra and a kshetrajna (field and knower of the field), when it comes to jnana or knowledge, there are three aspects:

Jnana is the knowledge.
Jneyam is the object of knowledge (what is to be known).
Jneta is the knower of this knowledge.

All these are always together.

So far, Shri Krishna has categorized kshetra, kshetrajna, and jnana. Next, He categorizes jneyam.

ज्ञेयं यत्तत्प्रवक्ष्यामि यज्ज्ञात्वामृतमश्नुते ।
अनादिमत्परं ब्रह्म न सत्तन्नासदुच्यते ॥१३-१२॥

jñeyaṃ yat tat pravakṣyāmi yaj jñātvāmṛtam aśnute I
anādimat paraṃ brahma na sat tan nāsad ucyate II13-12II

I shall now describe what is to be known, knowing which, one can attain immortality, the Supreme Brahman which is called neither being nor non-being.

We need to first cultivate humility and the required virtues and become a jnani (a person who is well versed in jnana, more simply, a knowledgeable person) in order to fully comprehend the jneyam (the object of knowledge).

One key aspect which is beautifully explained by Swami Ranganathananda is that, in the material sciences, just by knowing the atom, the scientist does not become an atom. However, in the spiritual science, just by knowing the Brahman (God), you become Brahman (you merge into God).

As an example, consider that a block of rock salt wants to 'know' the salt in the ocean. It goes and takes a dip in the ocean. As soon as it spends a few seconds in the ocean, it starts to melt. Once it melts, it 'becomes' the ocean. So, by the time it 'realized' the salt in the ocean, it had become the ocean.

This profound truth expounded by Shri Krishna holds one of the secret keys to liberation.

Such is the nature of the absolute pure consciousness, the Brahman. **You can experience it, you can become one with it, but you cannot explain it.**

Inspired by Swami Vivekananda's summary (from the complete works of Swami Vivekananda, vol 1), I would like to lay down the summary of spiritual knowledge as follows:

1. Each soul is potentially divine.

2. The goal is to manifest this divine within. How? Refer to Shri Krishna's explanations covered so far and follow the commandments.
3. Realize this truth and be liberated. If you really want to 'know' the Brahman, then focus on and get a deep understanding of the qualities of jnana (knowledge) explained by Shri Krishna in this chapter.
4. Doctrines, dogmas, rituals, books, temples, forms are all secondary. What is primary is whether you are focusing on manifesting the divine within.

This body of ours is the kshetra (field). We think we are the masters of our own causes. However, we are merely fields, upon which other forces act upon. Shri Krishna says "know Me to be the kshetrajna of all kshetras". The Supreme Lord is the ultimate kshetrajna.

There is only one absolute 'kshetrajna' and 'jneta' although there are countless 'kshetras' (fields) and 'jneyams' (objects of knowledge).

समं पश्यन्हि सर्वत्र समवस्थितमीश्वरम् ।
न हिनस्त्यात्मनात्मानं ततो याति परां गतिम् ॥ १३-२८ ॥

samaṃ paśyan hi sarvatra samavasthitam īśvaram |
na hinasty ātmanātmānaṃ tato yāti parāṃ gatim ||13-28||

Seeing that the same Brahman (supreme soul) is present everywhere and in everyone equally, He or She abstains from injuring/harming the self by the self and so goes to the highest goal.

In this extremely logical manner, Shri Krishna provides another perspective on the importance of non-violence. If the same Brahman exists in you and me, what either of us experience is ultimately experienced by the ultimate Brahman. So, we should not cause harm or hurt to anyone.

Commandment 12:

Abandon ego. Approach knowledge with humility. Knowing God is possible only then.

Commandment 13:

Know that God exists in everyone, so harm no one.

CHAPTER 14
The Three Modes Of Nature

This chapter deals with the three modes of nature termed as gunas[34]. The three gunas are:

1. **Sattva/ Sattvic** (goodness, constructive, harmonious)
2. **Rajas/Rajasic** (based on passion, tendency to be confusing)
3. **Tamas/Tamasic** (badness, darkness, ignorance, destructive, chaotic)

All these gunas are present in different proportions in everything that you can see and feel in the universe.

So far, Sri Krishna has spoken about so many different aspects of action, inaction, devotion, detachment, humility, knowledge, field, knower of the field, etc. Here in this chapter, He explains how these three gunas form the basis of and the root cause behind everything that we are and that we do.

A careful study, understanding, and mastery over these gunas are essential and key to success and liberation. **According to Lord Krishna, liberation is possible even by just gaining mastery and control over the gunas within us.**

---

34 Gunas are the three modes of nature and forms the basis of all thoughts and actions

You can make the transition and evolve from the state of a kshetra to that of a kshetrajna by mastering this (yoga of mastery over the three gunas).

सत्त्वं रजस्तम इति गुणाः प्रकृतिसंभवाः ।
निबध्नन्ति महाबाहो देहे देहिनमव्ययम् ॥ १४-५ ॥

sattvaṃ rajas tama iti guṇāḥ prakṛtisaṃbhavāḥ I
nibadhnanti mahābāho dehe dehinam avyayam II14-5II

O mighty-armed one, the gunas of sattva, rajas, and tamas, born of prakriti (nature), bind the eternal living entity (purusha) to this body.

Prakriti is the manifested nature. Purusha is the force, the super soul, and spirit that keeps the universe in motion. Prakriti is the kshetra (field) while Purusha is the kshetrajna (knower of the field).

What you do and who you are, depends on which gunas are active and in what proportion within you. You are basically controlled by your gunas.

Every artist and computer science professional knows that we can create millions of shades and colors by mixing just three basic colors of Red, Green, and Blue. I remember as a young computer science student, how intrigued and excited I was to see the seemingly endless shades and colors I could create using a combination of just three colors! When Red, Green, and Blue are all set to 0, you get black. When you set all of them to the maximum possible value, you get white. These are two ends of the spectrum.

This is the distinction between 'nirguna[35]' (no gunas) and 'saguna' (all the gunas). The manifested God is understood to be 'saguna[36]' Brahman. The un-manifested, impersonal God is theorized to be 'nirguna' Brahman. Both ends of the spectrum culminate in the Supreme Brahman.

---

35 nirguna means 'having no gunas or attributeless'

36 Saguna means 'having all the gunas or all possible attributes'

Everything in the known universe lies in between. Everything you can perceive with your senses and even those that you cannot, consist of different permutations of the three fundamental gunas.

What you do and who you are, depends on which gunas are active and in what proportion within you. Your thoughts and actions are manifestations of your gunas.

People who have more of rajasic and tamasic gunas in them will not have an inclination to know the divine or seek spiritual knowledge.

सत्त्वं सुखे सञ्जयति रजः कर्मणि भारत ।
ज्ञानमावृत्य तु तमः प्रमादे सञ्जयत्युत ॥ १४-९ ॥

sattvaṃ sukhe sañjayati rajaḥ karmaṇi bhārata ।
jñānam āvṛtya tu tamaḥ pramāde sañjayaty uta ॥14-9॥

Sattva attaches a person to joy, rajas to action, while tamas puts a veil on your intellect and attaches you to chaos and madness.

In the next few verses, Lord Krishna explains that at the time of your death, whichever of these gunas are predominant in you, determines what happens to you after death and where you will be reborn if you still haven't earned your liberation.

Thus, the gunas within you not only orchestrate your life but also has a direct impact on your afterlife.

A point to be noted is that prakriti (nature) works on principles and laws. For example, light travels at the speed of 300 thousand kilometers per second, no matter what the source of the light is. A magnet always aligns with the north and south poles, no matter who is holding the magnet. **Similarly, the gunas in you will determine the quality of your life no matter who you are.**

Prakriti will ensure this. If you want a good life (and afterlife), you have to cultivate good gunas and subdue the bad gunas. No exceptions and no escape from this.

नान्यं गुणेभ्यः कर्तारं यदा द्रष्टानुपश्यति ।
गुणेभ्यश्च परं वेत्ति मद्भावं सो ऽधिगच्छति ॥ १४-१९ ॥

nānyaṃ guṇebhyaḥ kartāraṃ yadā draṣṭānupaśyati ।
guṇebhyaś ca paraṃ vetti madbhāvaṃ so 'dhigacchati ॥14-19॥

When the seer sees that it is nothing else other than the gunas that are the agents of all action and when the seer is able to know the self which is higher than the gunas, he or she attains My state of being.

It is very important for us to observe and understand that it is the gunas that are constantly manipulating us. We should then try to realize that our higher self is beyond these gunas. Achieving that realization should be everyone's goal in life.

We have to constantly strive to rid ourselves of tamas and raise ourselves from rajas to sattva. Once we are fully in the mode of **sattva, we need to get rid of that as well**. Knowing that the Supreme Brahman is above and beyond all gunas.

Once you have risen above all your gunas and identified yourself with the Brahman within you, liberation will be achieved.

We should devote our entire life to raising ourselves higher. We need to realize that we are all puppets who are manipulated by the gunas. Once that happens, whenever we are unhappy with someone's behavior or actions, we will be able to focus more on the problem rather than the person.

Commandment 14

Focus on the problem and not the person. The gunas are the real culprits.

One of the gurus I have interacted within the past, Bal Govind Prabhu from Pune[37], had a simple formula to cultivate and maintain positive gunas by way of devotion and association. He used to call this formula 'ABCD'.

A for 'association'. Choose good people and spend time in their company.

B for 'books'. Read good books, holy scriptures like Bhagavad Gita.

C for 'chanting'. Practice chanting the name of God.

D for 'diet'. Avoid tamasic food. Follow a sattvic diet and stay away from all types of intoxicants.

That's it! He used to say. Cultivating good gunas is as simple as ABCD ☺

37 Pune is a city in the state of Maharashtra. It is considered to be the education capital of India as it has the most number of educational institutions compared with any other state.

CHAPTER 15

Pathway To The Supreme Spirit

निर्मानमोहा जितसङ्गदोषा अध्यात्मनित्या विनिवृत्तकामाः ।
द्वंद्वैर्विमुक्ताः सुखदुःखसंज्ञैर्
  गच्छन्त्यमूढाः पदमव्ययं तत् ॥ १५-५ ॥

nirmānamohā jitasaṅgadoṣā; adhyātmanityā vinivṛttakāmāḥ I ||15-5||
dvaṃdvair vimuktāḥ sukhaduḥkhasaṃjñair; gacchanty amūḍhāḥ padam avyayaṃ tat

Those who are free from pride and delusion, who have vanquished the evil of attachment, ever abiding in the self, who have stilled all desires, who are freed from the pairs of opposites known as pleasure & pain, they reach undeluded, the eternal goal of that imperishable Brahman.

ममैवांशो जीवलोके जीवभूतः सनातनः ।
मनःषष्ठानीन्द्रियाणि प्रकृतिस्थानि कर्षति ॥ १५-७ ॥

mamaivāṃśo jīvaloke jīvabhūtaḥ sanātanaḥ I
manaḥṣaṣṭhānīndriyāṇi prakṛtisthāni karṣati ||15-7||

A fragment of my eternal self, having become a living soul in the world of the living (prakriti), draws to itself from external nature, the five senses with the mind as the sixth.

Lord Krishna here confirms that certainly, it is a spark of His eternal self only which is embodied in all living beings. That's what makes it the ultimate goal, of getting reunited with that eternal soul or Brahman.

As we have seen earlier, Lord Krishna has explained the concept of Purusha and prakriti. Prakriti is the kshetra (field) while Purusha[38] is the kshetrajna (knower of the field).

Lord Krishna further says that there is a super soul or 'Uttama Purusha', the perfect, singular soul.

He is the 'Uttama Purusha'. He is both, saguna (having all qualities) and nirguna (devoid of any qualities). He is beyond comprehension.

Throughout the Gita, Sri Krishna has reiterated that only humans have the ability to realize this truth and that realizing this truth should be the ultimate goal of all humans.

Lord Krishna concludes this chapter thus:

इति गुह्यतमं शास्त्रमिदमुक्तं मयानघ ।
एतद्बुद्ध्वा बुद्धिमान्स्यात्कृतकृत्यश्च भारत ॥ १५-२० ॥

iti guhyatamaṃ śāstram idam uktaṃ mayānagha I
etad buddhvā buddhimān syāt kṛtakṛtyaś ca bhārata II15-20II

Thus, O sinless one, this most profound science has been imparted by Me. Knowing this, one attains the highest intelligence and will have accomplished all one's duties, O descendant of Bharatha!

38 Purusa and Purusha both mean the same thing

CHAPTER 16

Divine And Non-Divine Attributes Of Humans

All positive human tendencies can be attributed to 'daivi' (moral, divine) nature and all negative tendencies can be attributed to 'asuri' (immoral, demoniac) nature. In this chapter, Sri Krishna explains the classification and also stresses the importance of aligning with the moral and daivik aspects in our daily life.

अभयं सत्त्वसंशुद्धिर्ज्ञानयोगव्यवस्थितिः ।
दानं दमश्च यज्ञश्च स्वाध्यायस्तप आर्जवम् ॥१६-१॥

abhayaṃ sattvasaṃśuddhir jñānayogavyavasthitiḥ ।
dānaṃ damaś ca yajñaś ca svādhyāyas tapa ārjavam ॥16-1॥

Fearlessness, purity of heart, steadfastness in knowledge & yoga, almsgiving, control of the senses, Yajna (sacrifice), the study of the spiritual texts, austerity, uprightness.

Sri Krishna explains the qualities of moral and daivik people. He starts the list with the quality of 'fearlessness' (abhayam). This is a very important quality and a pre-requisite for other qualities to survive and thrive.

One of the reasons why saintly people are usually alone whereas crooks and demoniac people always move around in groups or gangs is because when you do good, think good, feel good, your higher self will automatically pull your consciousness higher up (the result of your sattvic gunas). Fear is a lower (tamasic) guna and it disappears when you are in the higher realms of consciousness.

Whereas, if you do bad, think bad, think negative, your consciousness will get drawn further down where lower emotions like fear and anger thrive. Thus, you land up becoming more and more fearful deep within you. Having many people around you provides a false sense of security. People who constantly feel fear in their hearts need this sense of security to compensate for the deep sense of insecurity that they have within themselves.

The true and real sense of security is when you feel fearless within. Only a sattvic life can give you that. Another important point to note is that **both daivi, as well as asuri qualities, have a tendency of pulling you further and further in their respective directions.**

Regardless of how low you are feeling, **if you want to raise yourself higher, just start with one good thought or one good deed**. Be consistent. Very soon you will find yourself thinking more good thoughts and doing more good deeds. That is the magic of prakriti in action. Your one good thought and one good deed causes the good gunas to start pulling your inner self higher up in their direction.

The converse is also true. No matter how good or saintly you are, one bad thought and one bad deed has the potential to draw you further down and you can fall into disgrace very quickly.

This is the law of prakriti (universe). It never fails.

Now, you need to be fearless to defend and grow your good qualities and you need to consistently follow the good path in order to become more and more fearless.

No matter what the level of your consciousness is, you can either take it higher or lower. It is usually fear (or lack of fear) that determines which way you go.

I was once walking with an acquaintance in the scenic streets of Vancouver. We came across a Buddhist monk who was peacefully seeking for help and saying that he has no money. I knew that the person walking with me had a lot of money on him so I whispered to him if he would like to donate something to this monk. He refused and he told me that members of his community will get upset with him if they found out that he helped someone from another religious community.

You see, this person wanted to be good and do good. But then there was this fear of social acceptance that was preventing him from doing good.

The irony is that it is mostly the good people who have to face their fears of social acceptance. Because the bad guys are usually in a group and they don't feel the need for social acceptance beyond that group. They go around doing bad deeds with the false sense of belonging that they have.

If we can analyze and understand this, it will become clearer why fearlessness is a key requirement for being good and treading on the path of goodness.

As famously said by Dale Carnegie[39]: "If you want to conquer fear, don't sit home and think about it. Go out and get busy."

अहिंसा सत्यमक्रोधस्त्यागः शान्तिरपैशुनम् ।
दया भूतेष्वलोलुप्त्वं मार्दवं ह्रीरचापलम् ॥ १६-२ ॥

ahiṃsā satyam akrodhas tyāgaḥ śāntir apaiśunam I
dayā bhūteṣv aloluptvaṃ mārdavaṃ hrīr acāpalam II16-2II

Non-violence, truthfulness, freedom from anger, renunciation, tranquility, aversion to faultfinding, compassion, non-covetousness, gentleness, modesty, steady-mindedness.

---

39 Dale Carnegie was an American writer and lecturer. One of his most famous quotes was 'remember that today is the tomorrow that you worried about yesterday'

तेजः क्षमा धृतिः शौचमद्रोहो नातिमानिता ।
भवन्ति संपदं दैवीमभिजातस्य भारत ॥ १६-३ ॥

tejaḥ kṣamā dhṛtiḥ śaucam adroho nātimānitā I
bhavanti saṃpadaṃ daivīm abhijātasya bhārata II16-3II

Vigor, forgiveness, fortitude, cleanliness, freedom from envy, passion for honor. These transcendental qualities belong to daivi and Godly men endowed with divine nature.

Lord Krishna again speaks about the importance of non-violence here. If you are afraid of your opponent and you run away that is cowardice, not non-violence. But if you believe you are stronger and capable of hurting your opponent and you choose to not cause any harm, that is true non-violence.

Only the fearless and strong are capable of non-violence.

Non-violence is also attributed to 'gentleness'. Elsewhere in the Mahabharata, the virtues of gentleness are explained (III.29.30).

Mrduna mardavam hanti,
Mrduna hanti darunam.
Na asadhyam mrduna kincit,
Tasmat tiksnataro mrduh.

Meaning:

The gentle conquers the gentle,
The gentle conquers the hard.
There is nothing that gentleness cannot gain,
Gentleness is the most powerful thing,
The most penetrating thing.

Water flowing in streams is so soft and gentle. However, it is a well-documented fact that a gentle, flowing stream of water has cut through mountains and created pathways through the toughest of terrains. The mighty and awe-inspiring Grand Canyon in Arizona has been created by the constantly flowing Colorado river. A gentle river that carved a canyon through solid rock, over 6000 feet deep and stretching over 400 kilometers!!

Commandment 15

Be fearless. Be gentle. Be strong. These are essential for Goodness to thrive.

Lord Krishna then continues to explain and classify the demoniac (bad, negative) qualities.

दम्भो दर्पो ऽतिमानश्च क्रोधः पारुष्यमेव च ।
अज्ञानं चाभिजातस्य पार्थ संपदमासुरीम् ॥ १६-४ ॥

dambho darpo 'timānaś ca krodhaḥ pāruṣyam eva ca |
ajñānaṃ cābhijātasya pārtha saṃpadam āsurīm ||16-4||

Pride, arrogance, self-importance, anger, harshness, and ignorance belong to those of demoniac nature.

प्रवृत्तिं च निवृत्तिं च जना न विदुरासुराः ।
न शौचं नापि चाचारो न सत्यं तेषु विद्यते ॥ १६-७ ॥

pravṛttiṃ ca nivṛttiṃ ca janā na vidur āsurāḥ ।
na śaucaṃ nāpi cācāro na satyaṃ teṣu vidyate ॥16-7॥

The person of demoniac nature knows not what to do and what not to do (refrain from). Neither is purity found in them nor good conduct nor truth.

आशापाशशतैर्बद्धाः कामक्रोधपरायणाः ।
ईहन्ते कामभोगार्थमन्यायेनार्थसंचयान् ॥ १६-१२ ॥

āśāpāśaśatair baddhāḥ kāmakrodhaparāyaṇāḥ ।
īhante kāmabhogārtham anyāyenārthasaṃcayān ॥16-12॥

Bound by hundreds of ties of desire, addicted to lust and anger, they seek to amass riches by unjust means, with the sole purpose of gratifying their senses.

आसुरीं योनिमापन्ना मूढा जन्मनि जन्मनि ।
मामप्राप्यैव कौन्तेय ततो यान्त्यधमां गतिम् ॥ १६-२० ॥

āsurīṃ yonim āpannā mūḍhā janmani janmani ।
mām aprāpyaiva kaunteya tato yānty adhamāṃ gatim ॥16-20॥

Obtaining the demoniac wombs and deluded, birth after birth, not attaining Me, they thus fall, O son of Kunti, into a still lower condition.

As explained earlier, negative gunas have a cyclic effect, dragging the person lower and lower.

Sri Krishna is reiterating the fact here by saying that people of demoniac nature keep taking birth through demoniac wombs and keep falling lower and lower, never reaching Him.

त्रिविधं नरकस्येदं द्वारं नाशनमात्मनः ।
कामः क्रोधस्तथा लोभस्तस्मादेतत्त्रयं त्यजेत् ॥ १६-२१ ॥

trividhaṃ narakasyedaṃ dvāraṃ nāśanam ātmanaḥ I
kāmaḥ krodhas tathā lobhas tasmād etat trayaṃ tyajet ॥16-21॥

There are three gateways to hell and self-destruction. Lust, anger, and greed. Therefore, one should abandon and forsake these qualities.

Sri Krishna has disclosed many secrets for going to higher states and achieving liberation. In this verse, he discloses a profound secret about what the three fundamental and major paths to downfall are, which we should all avoid at all cost. Those being **lust, anger, and greed**.

In this chapter, Sri Krishna has very objectively explained all the demoniac as well as Godly qualities. We just have to stop engaging in demoniac thoughts and actions and start/continue inculcating daivi/Godly thoughts and engaging in good deeds. That is a constant endeavor that we must all undertake.

Commandment 16

Abandon lust, anger, and greed. These are the gateways to hell.

CHAPTER 17
Mind Over Matter

This chapter deals with human life and activities in the context of the gunas (sattva, rajas, and tamas). This is a careful study of the human mind and the forces acting upon the mind.

यजन्ते सात्त्विका देवान्यक्षरक्षांसि राजसाः ।
प्रेतान्भूतगणांश्चान्ये यजन्ते तामसा जनाः ॥ १७-४ ॥

yajante sāttvikā devān yakṣarakṣāṃsi rājasāḥ ।
pretān bhūtagaṇāṃś cānye yajante tāmasā janāḥ ॥17-4॥

The sattvic or the pure men worship the gods or devas; the rajasic or the passionate worship the yakshas and the rakshasas; The tamasic or the deluded people worship the ghosts and other lowly spirits.

Devas = Godly beings.
Yakshas, Rakshasas = Demoniac entities.
Pretas, Bhutas = ghosts, dead bodies, and human spirits.

In the next two verses, Sri Krishna says that there are people who perform severe austerities not recommended by the spiritual scriptures, in a mindset of ego and impelled by the force of desire and passion.

They senselessly torture all the organs in the body and the higher soul that is residing inside them. We should know them to be of asurik (demoniac) nature.

आहारस्त्वपि सर्वस्य त्रिविधो भवति प्रियः ।
यज्ञस्तपस्तथा दानं तेषां भेदमिमं शृणु ॥ १७-७ ॥

āhāras tv api sarvasya trividho bhavati priyaḥ ।
yajñas tapas tathā dānaṃ teṣāṃ bhedam imaṃ śṛṇu ॥17-7॥

The food which is dear to all is of three types, so are the sacrifices, austerities, and charity.

This is a very important distinction. Even seemingly good acts are of different types. Acts that 'look' good may not be necessarily good as they may be performed with ulterior motives.

The key teaching here is that regardless of what you are thinking or doing, keep a check on your mind. Make sure that your mind is always aligned with the sattvic guna.

Don't focus on just the actions. Focus also on the mindset behind your actions.

Now Sri Krishna classifies the food we consume based on the gunas.

आयुःसत्त्वबलारोग्यसुखप्रीतिविवर्धनाः ।
रस्याः स्निग्धाः स्थिरा हृद्या आहाराः सात्त्विकप्रियाः ॥ १७-८ ॥

āyuḥsattvabalārogyasukhaprītivivardhanāḥ ।
rasyāḥ snigdhāḥ sthirā hṛdyā āhārāḥ sāttvikapriyāḥ ॥17-8॥

The foods which increase vitality, purity, strength, health, joy and cheerfulness and appetite, which are savory, not too dry, substantial and agreeable, are dear to the sattvic people.

कट्वम्ललवणात्युष्णतीक्ष्णरूक्षविदाहिनः ।
आहारा राजसस्येष्टा दुःखशोकामयप्रदाः ॥ १७-९ ॥

kaṭvamlalavaṇātyuṣṇatīkṣṇarūkṣavidāhinaḥ ।
āhārā rājasasyeṣṭā duḥkhaśokāmayapradāḥ ॥17-9॥

The foods that are bitter, sour, very salty, excessively hot, pungent, dry and burning, are liked by the rajasic people and cause pain, grief, and disease.

यातयामं गतरसं पूति पर्युषितं च यत् ।
उच्छिष्टमपि चामेध्यं भोजनं तामसप्रियम् ॥ १७-१० ॥

yātayāmaṃ gatarasaṃ pūti paryuṣitaṃ ca yat ।
ucchiṣṭam api cāmedhyaṃ bhojanaṃ tāmasapriyam ॥17-10॥

Food which is stale, tasteless, putrid, rotten and impure, is liked by the tamasic people.

In the next few verses, Sri Krishna explains that sacrifices, austerities, and charities are all worthy and sattvic when performed with a mindset of humility, devotion and without any attachment to the fruits.

We have looked at the classification of food and actions based on gunas. Now we will see the classification of speech.

अनुद्वेगकरं वाक्यं सत्यं प्रियहितं च यत् ।
स्वाध्यायाभ्यसनं चैव वाङ्मयं तप उच्यते ॥ १७-१५ ॥

anudvegakaraṃ vākyaṃ satyaṃ priyahitaṃ ca yat ।
svādhyāyābhyasanaṃ caiva vāṅmayaṃ tapa ucyate ॥17-15॥

Speech which causes no agitation, which is truthful, pleasant and beneficial, and practicing self-study is called austerity of speech.

Our words and speech are very powerful and have a huge impact on ourselves and the lives of others. The ancient Toltecs [40]laid down four agreements to abide by for a meaningful and successful life. The first and foremost agreement was "**Be impeccable with your word**".

To do bodily harm to someone, you have to be physically strong yourself. And when you physically harm someone, the chances are high that you will incur some damage yourself. However, even a very feeble person can say harsh or very negative words that totally destroy the other person. Just a few words can create havoc in society. If used correctly, words can also do a lot of good. It can build a person's confidence, make someone feel loved, impart wisdom to others, etc. And in the holy Bible, it says "In the beginning was the Word, and the Word was with God, and the Word was God". Such is the importance of words. So be very careful which ones you use and make it your constant endeavor to always use sattvic words and speech.

मनःप्रसादः सौम्यत्वं मौनमात्मविनिग्रहः ।
भावसंशुद्धिरित्येतत्तपो मानसमुच्यते ॥ १७-१६ ॥

manaḥprasādaḥ saumyatvaṃ maunam ātmavinigrahaḥ I
bhāvasaṃśuddhir ity etat tapo mānasam ucyate II17-16II

The serenity of mind, kindness, silence, self-control, purity of nature. This is called austerity of the mind.

Thus, we have covered the threefold austerities (physical, mental and verbal). It is important to practice these consistently. It is also important that we practice these without expectations of benefits and with complete faith in the Lord. That is the path to liberation.

---

40 The Toltecs were an ancient civilization revered by both, the Mayans as well as the Aztecs.

Commandment 17

Always be mindful of your words. Choose to be silent if you have nothing good to say.

CHAPTER 18
The Way Of Liberation

At a high level, the first six chapters focus on karma yoga, the next six on bhakti yoga and the last six on jnana yoga. In this 18th chapter, Shri Krishna summarizes everything He has said in the first 17 chapters and adds some more details about liberation. Because He touches upon most of the things He has said till now, this is the longest chapter in the Bhagavad Gita with 78 verses. The second longest chapter is right at the beginning, chapter 2 with 72 verses where Shri Krishna lays down the strong foundation for everything else that He is going to say in the subsequent chapters. That is why as you can see, the most number of commandments have been derived from chapter 2.

Spiritual knowledge is subjective and most of the times, it has to be applied based on context. For example, assume that you are a saint sitting under a tree in a forest when a man comes running to you saying "can you help me as some robbers are trying to kill me?". You then ask him to go hide inside the old well behind your hut. Soon the robbers come that way and ask you if you have seen anyone come running this way. What would you do? Do you tell them that he is hiding in the well because the scriptures say that you should always speak the truth? Or do you send the robbers on a different path because the scriptures tell you to be compassionate and prevent causing harm to anyone?

Just like this, you will face many situations in life where you have to decide the right course of action based upon the context. That is the reason Shri Krishna has used 700 verses to pass on the knowledge to Arjuna (and humanity) instead of just dictating what you should and should not do. The bulk of these verses are providing us with the context and instructions to improve our wisdom so that we can decide what situations need to be handled how. That is the difference between knowledge and wisdom.

There is a famous saying in Italy that goes like "the smart man knows how to pull the trigger, whereas the wise man knows when to pull the trigger".

It is natural for us to keep having questions in our mind on what is the most appropriate course of action for any given context. Arjuna had many such questions like 'is it better to work or give up work?', 'is it better to be engaged in the world or is it better to become a sannyasi (renunciation)?', 'is it better to do bhakti yoga or is it better to do jnana yoga?' etc. and Shri Krishna has answered all his questions categorically and logically for the benefit of all of humanity.

In this chapter, Shri Krishna answers all remaining questions apart from summarizing whatever He has said in the previous 17 chapters.

यज्ञदानतपःकर्म न त्याज्यं कार्यमेव तत् ।
यज्ञो दानं तपश्चैव पावनानि मनीषिणाम् ॥१८-५॥

yajñadānatapaḥkarma na tyājyaṃ kāryam eva tat I
yajño dānaṃ tapaś caiva pāvanāni manīṣiṇām II18-5II

एतान्यपि तु कर्माणि सङ्गं त्यक्त्वा फलानि च ।
कर्तव्यानीति मे पार्थ निश्चितं मतमुत्तमम् ॥ १८-६ ॥

etāny api tu karmāṇi saṅgaṃ tyaktvā phalāni ca ।
kartavyānīti me pārtha niścitaṃ matam uttamam ॥18-6॥

Acts of sacrifice, charity and austerity should not be abandoned but should be performed, for these are the purifiers of even the wise and great souls

But even these actions should be performed without attachment and the desire for rewards, O Arjuna, this is My certain and ultimate conviction.

As you may recall, this verse is a recap of verse 2.47 which said "*You are entitled to (or have a right to) perform rightful actions. But you are never entitled to the fruits of your action. Never be motivated by the fruits of actions nor be attached to inaction.*"

न हि देहभृता शक्यं त्यक्तुं कर्माण्यशेषतः ।
यस्तु कर्मफलत्यागी स त्यागीत्यभिधीयते ॥ १८-११ ॥

na hi dehabhṛtā śakyaṃ tyaktuṃ karmāṇy aśeṣataḥ ।
yas tu karmaphalatyāgī sa tyāgīty abhidhīyate ॥18-11॥

It is not possible for an embodied being to relinquish actions entirely, but one who relinquishes the fruits of actions is verily called a 'Tyagi' (man of renunciation).

पञ्चैतानि महाबाहो कारणानि निबोध मे ।
सांख्ये कृतान्ते प्रोक्तानि सिद्धये सर्वकर्मणाम् ॥ १८-१३ ॥

pañcaitāni mahābāho kāraṇāni nibodha me ।
sāṃkhye kṛtānte proktāni siddhaye sarvakarmaṇām ॥18-13॥

Learn from Me, O mighty-armed Arjuna, the following five causes as declared in the Samkhya system for the accomplishment of all actions.

The Samkhya philosophers were astute thinkers. They were ancient scientists, philosophers as well as psychologists. The first among them was Maharishi Kapila[41], who established the Samkhya system.

Lord Krishna makes a reference to this system and calls out that there it has been established that there are five causes of every action. He then explains what those five causes are.

अधिष्ठानं तथा कर्ता करणं च पृथग्विधम् ।
विविधाश्च पृथक्चेष्टा दैवं चैवात्र पञ्चमम् ॥ १८-१४ ॥

adhiṣṭhānaṃ tathā kartā karaṇaṃ ca pṛthagvidham ।
vividhāś ca pṛthakceṣṭā daivaṃ caivātra pañcamam ॥18-14॥

The place of action (body), the doer, the various senses, the different processes of action, and ultimately, the divine soul within you. These are the five factors of action.

Whatever actions, whether right or wrong that a human performs is caused by these five factors. A key takeaway here is that a person should never get into the mindset of 'I am the doer or cause of action', because there are actually these five factors that actually determine what you do or don't do. Not to mention that four out of these five factors (except the ultimate divine soul within us) are themselves driven by the three gunas.

---

41 Maharishi Kapila is a Vedic sage (rishi) traditionally considered to be the original proponent of the Samkhya system of Indian philosophy. He is said to have lived in the Indian subcontinent, around the sixth or seventh century B.C.E

ज्ञानं ज्ञेयं परिज्ञाता त्रिविधा कर्मचोदना ।
करणं कर्म कर्तेति त्रिविधः कर्मसंग्रहः ॥१८-१८॥

jñānaṃ jñeyaṃ parijñātā trividhā karmacodanā ।
karaṇaṃ karma karteti trividhaḥ karmasaṃgrahaḥ ॥18-18॥

Knowledge (jnana), the object of knowledge (jneyam) and the knower (jneta) form the threefold impulse to action. While the instrument, the object acted upon, and the agent of action (actor), form the threefold constituents of action.

Earlier, Shri Krishna had explained how knowledge, action and the agent of action all can have different gunas associated with them (sattvic, rajasic or tamasic). As you can see, there is a lot involved in your actions & the karma you generate. It is necessary to contemplate upon all these various aspects.

As an example, if your car has a flat tire, you know how to fix it. But if you drive over the same nail again, you will again land up with a flat tire. So, a mindset of 'if there is a flat tire, this is how you fix it' is helpful only in the short term. In the long run, you need to understand the root cause(s) and resolve them in order to prevent having flat tires in future.

Likewise, just forcing a change your actions is not sufficient. You need to understand all the various aspects of your actions and resolve them in order to make sure that your actions remain aligned with the sattvic and the divine. This is the way to get liberation from the Karmic cycle of cause and effect.

An extremely potent and ominous verse follows.

स्वभावजेन कौन्तेय निबद्धः स्वेन कर्मणा ।
कर्तुं नेच्छसि यन्मोहात्करिष्यस्यवशो ऽपि तत् ॥१८-६०॥

svabhāvajena kaunteya nibaddhaḥ svena karmaṇā ।
kartuṃ necchasi yan mohāt kariṣyasy avaśo 'pi tat ॥18-60॥

O son of Kunti, bound by your own karma, born of your own nature, what you, out of delusion desire not to do, you shall have to do in spite of yourself.

Lord Krishna says that based on your karma and your nature (mindset), you will be having to perform certain actions and duties. But out of delusion, if you try to avoid or ignore those actions and duties, then the cosmos or prakriti will force you to perform those actions and duties and you will eventually be doing it without your own wish and will.

You either do your duties willingly, humbly, without attachment or you land up having to do them forcefully. Your choice is only in deciding how you want to perform your duties. Whether you want to do your duties or not is never an option. This is one of the absolute laws of prakriti. So, the first thing is for us to understand well what our duties are and then make sure we do them with love, dedicating the actions to the Lord and not being attached to the results. If we can do that, we would have already removed most of the pain from our lives and begun the journey towards spiritual success, liberation, and attainment of the Supreme Lord.

As Kennedy [42]famously said, "Ask not what the country can do for you, but ask what you can do for your country". The actual message we should take away from this is that under every circumstance, we should first think about what our duties are, what and how we should be contributing. This paradigm shift in our thinking can bring an enormous transformation into our lives.

---

42 John F Kennedy was the 35th president of the USA

Commandment 18

Never ignore your duties. Performing your duties is the first step towards liberation.

अध्येष्यते च य इमं धर्म्यं संवादमावयोः ।
ज्ञानयज्ञेन तेनाहमिष्टः स्यामिति मे मतिः ॥ १८-७० ॥

adhyeṣyate ca ya imaṃ dharmyaṃ saṃvādam āvayoḥ ।
jñānayajñena tenāham iṣṭaḥ syām iti me matiḥ ॥18-70॥

One who will study this sacred dialogue of ours, conducive to social stability & enrichment, by that person shall I be worshipped by the Yajna [43] *of wisdom. Such is My conviction.*

The Lord has said here that he who studies this dialogue between Him and Arjuna is very dear to Him. That is what has been my humble endeavor, to study and help my brethren globally to get interested and participate in this study, enrich their lives, achieve spiritual success and become dear to God.

श्रद्धावाननसूयश्च शृणुयादपि यो नरः ।
सो ऽपि मुक्तः शुभांल्लोकान्प्राप्नुयात्पुण्यकर्मणाम् ॥ १८-७१ ॥

śraddhāvān anasūyaś ca śṛṇuyād api yo naraḥ ।
so 'pi muktaḥ śubhāṃl lokān prāpnuyāt puṇyakarmaṇām ॥18-71॥

And even that person who hears this (or just reads this), full of faith and free from malice, he, too shall be liberated and attain the happy worlds of those of righteous deeds.

Thus it is my humble request for you to read this work multiple times and become dear to God and attain liberation.

God bless!

---

43 Yajna literally means sacrifice, devotion, worship and offering

Summaries

The Commandments

1. Recognize the saboteur within you. Don't give into it. Confront it and vanquish it.
2. A calm mind is essential for achieving liberation. Learn to handle both pain and pleasure calmly.
3. Always choose rightful action over inaction. Never be attached to the results of your work.
4. Let thoughts of God & service to God replace your thoughts of sensory pleasures.
5. Know that lust is the root cause of all evil. Replace it with divine love for God.
6. Worship the Supreme God and worship solely out of love, never to gain something.
7. Destroy self-doubt. Your conviction in God depends upon your conviction in yourself.
8. Be committed and consistent with yoga. Vanquish your vikaras. You will find God then.
9. Control the mind by practicing moderation in eating, sleeping, working, and recreation.
10. Seeing God in everything and everyone, practice devotion and humility consistently.

11. Be compassionate and do not have hatred towards any living being.
12. Abandon ego. Approach knowledge with humility. Knowing God is possible only then.
13. Know that God exists in everyone, so harm no one.
14. Focus on the problem and not the person. The gunas are the real culprits.
15. Be fearless. Be gentle. Be strong. These are essential for Goodness to thrive.
16. Abandon lust, anger, and greed. These are the gateways to hell.
17. Always be mindful of your words. Choose to be silent if you have nothing good to say.
18. Never ignore your duties. Performing your duties is the first step towards liberation.

Foods: The good, bad and the ugly

Sattvic foods	Foods which increase vitality, purity, strength, health, joy and cheerfulness and appetite, which are savory, not too dry, substantial and agreeable.
Rajasic foods	Foods that are bitter, sour, very salty, excessively hot, pungent, dry and burning, are liked by the rajasic people and cause pain, grief, and disease.
Tamasic foods	Food which is stale, tasteless, putrid, rotten and impure, is liked by the tamasic people. These only destroy the body and cause serious diseases.

Devotion: The good, bad and the ugly

Sattvic qualities	The sattvic or the pure men worship the gods or devas.
Rajasic qualities	The rajasic or the passionate worship the yakshas and the rakshasas.
Tamasic qualities	The tamasic or the deluded people worship the ghosts and other lowly spirits.

Austerity of speech (how speech should be)

Speech which causes no agitation, which is truthful, pleasant and beneficial, and practicing self-study is called austerity of speech.

Austerity of mind (how the mind should be)

The serenity of mind, kindness, silence, self-control, purity of nature. This is called austerity of the mind.

Godly/daivik qualities

Fearlessness, purity of heart, steadfastness in knowledge & yoga, almsgiving, control of the senses, Yajna (sacrifice), the study of the spiritual texts, austerity, uprightness, vigor, forgiveness, fortitude, cleanliness, freedom from envy, passion for honor.

Demoniac/asurik qualities

Pride, arrogance, self-importance, anger, harshness, and ignorance belong to those of demoniac nature.

Classification of action

The place of action (body), the doer, the various senses, the different processes of action, and ultimately, the divine soul within you. These are the five factors of action.

Knowledge (jnana), the object of knowledge (jneyam) and the knower (jneta) form the threefold impulse to action. While the instrument, the object acted upon, and the agent of action (actor), form the threefold constituents of action.

A Glance At The Author

I was fortunate to have been born in a family of book lovers. I have spent most of my childhood surrounded by books, mostly pertaining to philosophy, spirituality, literature and science.

No matter how many books I read, the concept of God proved to be the most difficult to comprehend. There were so many questions in my mind and so few answers.

Is God a person or just a force? Does God really give a damn about us humans? Why does God let bad things happen to good people? Why do some people get success easily while others seem to struggle? Does it have anything to do with their God connection?

Am I free to live life like I wish or does God control every aspect of it? And many more...

I once came across this famous quote by Albert Einstein "*We cannot solve our problems with the same level of consciousness that created them*".

It made sense to me. If we consider God to be a higher force or superior being, then we cannot comprehend or explain God unless we are able to raise our level of consciousness. And most religious texts and scriptures have explained that the best way to connect with God is through devotion and surrender to God. Both are possible only for a humble mind and a loving heart.

With this humility, I set out to understand what exactly it means to 'surrender' to God. Does it mean I don't act or do anything at all? If not, how much should I do or act? How do I know whether my surrender is sufficient?

I spent years with these questions in my mind and searching for answers through meditation as well as by reading every piece of spiritual text I could lay my hands on, regardless of whether it was from the east or the west. I also spent a lot of time reading the works of Plato and Socrates who in my opinion are masters in the art of questioning (and answering them as well). At a very young age, I was greatly influenced by Swami Vivekananda's works. Two of his works impacted me most profoundly. One was his works on "bhakti yoga" and the other was on "karma yoga". These I have read multiple times and spent many years of my life trying to practice as much as I could.

My professional background is in the field of computer science and I have a knack for and experience in, solving complex problems and explaining the concepts in an analytical and structured manner. I have made a very humble attempt here in this book to use that experience and provide my analysis of this ancient scripture, focusing on actionable items that I am terming as 'commandments'.

There is a very famous saying in management 'if you can't measure it, you can't improve it'. If you want to grow on the spiritual path, it helps to have some way of measuring your success. Here, I have extracted 18 commandments from the Gita. At the least, we can always check how many of those we are able to follow in our own lives and use that as one of the measurements for our success on the spiritual plane.

+Vinayak Raghuvamshi
(Krsnadaasa)

References

Bhagavad Gita lectures by Swami Ranganathananda: http://www.rkmathharipad.org/video/bhagavad-gita-lectures-by-swami-ranganathanandaji/

Bhagavad Gita As-It-Is by Bhaktivedanta Swami Prabhupada: https://prabhupadabooks.com/bg

The Bhagavad Gita, a new translation, by Georg Feuerstein: ISBN 978-1-61180-038-8

The complete works of Swami Vivekananda: http://www.ramakrishnavivekananda.info/vivekananda/complete_works.htm

Sankaracharya's commentaries on the Bhagavad Gita: https://archive.org/details/Bhagavad-Gita.with.the.Commentary.of.Sri.Shankaracharya

Saint Kabir's two-line poems: https://en.wikipedia.org/wiki/Kabir

NOTES

NOTES

NOTES

NOTES

CPSIA information can be obtained
at www.ICGtesting.com
Printed in the USA
LVOW08s2010250118
563914LV00008B/65/P

9 781773 704333